APHRODITE'S PRIESTESS

APHRODITE'S PRIESTESS

LAURELEI BLACK

Asteria Books
Jeffersonville, Indiana

A publication of Asteria Books

631 Chestnut, Suite A, Jeffersonville, Indiana
47130

Printed in the United States of America

ISBN 1449964974

Book and cover design by Natalie Black

Cover image "Aphrodite on Swan" by Pistoxenos.
Copyright © Marie-Lan Ngyuen/Wikimedia Commons

CONTENTS

ACKNOWLEDGEMENTS

Several people have been highly instrumental in giving me the opportunity and space to explore the path of this particular Priestesshood, and I want to make clear to them how valued that support has always been. So a hundred-thousand thanks and kisses to my dear ex-husband, Scott, for giving and receiving love with me for so long; to Natalie and Joe, my partners in love, magic, writing, and life; Holly and Eric, my loving babes who remind me daily of Aphrodite's blessings as Mother; and Katie Ann, my best and truest friend. Also, many thanks to the Clan of the Laughing Dragon, Theorte Ekstasis, and the Qadishti Institute for all you have done and been in my life.

This work contains adult content. I do not recommend this book for children of any age due to its mature and sometimes sexual nature.

Furthermore, Greek Reconstructionists and practitioners of Hellenismos should please note that I make very little attempt to accurately reconstruct ancient temple practices or Greek customs in either this book or in my personal work. As a contemporary Priestess of Aphrodite, I feel at liberty to interpret Her mythos through a contemporary lens. Moreover, I am not inclined, in Her service, to be dogmatic or rigid in my approach to the sacred. I listen for Her (usually) gentle guidance and do my best to follow it.

I offer this book to the violet-crowned Kyprian as a work of love and adoration in Her honor, and to Her Priests and Priestesses in whatever ways they practice. May it open up the discussion and lead the way for more voices to speak and sing Her glory.

CHAPTER 1
HERE WE ARE

TURN TO ME, DEAR ONE, TURN THY FACE,
AND UNVEIL FOR ME IN THINE EYES, THEIR GRACE.

- SAPPHO

MY BACKGROUND

This is a conscious beginning. Like a babe who comes screaming into the world, I am aware that my voice will be heard, at least by some. Of those who hear the sounds of my new life, some will revel in the fresh awakening, the newness that it brings to their own lives. Some will see in these pages the first steps to their own rebirth. Others may well be offended by what, to them, is a cacophonous din of perversion and depravity.

I feel freed by my own determined effort to serve Aphrodite as her Priestess. I feel alive at the opportunity to share my explorations of this path through writing. I don't really intend that others will read these musings and decide to do what I have done as I have done it. This is not a handbook for the Cult of Aphrodite, it is more like a guide-book for the interested traveler down this path. I'm exploring my own theory and practice in working as Her devotee. I make no claims about having "the right way" to do anything. This work merely shows *my way* as it stands right now.

Let me begin by giving a brief explanation of how I got where I am. As rambling and long-winded as I can be, I prefer brevity on this particular part of the story.

My life leading up to my "calling" was a rather average American tale. I was brought up Baptist in the Midwest. Despite this rather conventional backdrop, my father instilled in me a very questioning spirit. I realized at 6 years old that I had some theological differences from the Baptist doctrine.

Yadda, yadda, yadda ... I grew up, got married at 19 (which was actually very uncommon given that I was in college in the late '90's), and then ... I had a spiritual awakening! I discovered Wicca. I found Paganism. I devoured everything that I could read about this religion. The Internet was relatively new, but it was filled with all manner of nifty tidbits – webpages filled with introductory materials, spells, message boards where I could ask all the newbie questions of folks just barely more experienced than myself.

I went through what was probably the common Solitary Wiccan experience in those first couple of years – trying to connect with people locally, reading the same five concepts spread out over 30 different book titles, journaling all my hopeful, neophyte ideas.

About two years passed, and I found myself living in the LA area, teaching English and Drama in the public high schools, expecting my first child (of two) and meeting the folks that would become my coven. I actually met them at the student ritual of one of the members. It was a Dionysian ritual, and it was absolutely liberating for me (in true Dionysian style). I knew I had found a spiritual home, and I bonded with the coven members very quickly.

The Clan of the Laughing Dragon has been fundamental in my spiritual development. That was the name of the coven at the time. That is now the name of the Tradition. At the time of this writing, we have two covens, and I am the High Priestess of the first daughter coven in the Tradition.

I know. I know. For those of you who don't particularly care about Pagan practice or Craft training (and related ideas of lineage and legitimacy), you're thinking, "Whoopty-doo." It's been a big deal to me, though. It took me seven years to go from the first day that I asked for membership until the day that my own coven was officially chartered into the Tradition. My High Priestess was a hard task-master, and I thank her for it. She was also the one who brought Aphrodite into my awareness.

For the record, I am just going to note that ours is not a Wiccan tradition. My former High Priestess, had Gardnerian, 1734, and Druidic training, but we don't make any effort to claim lineages through any of that work. What we do is a blend of some of those things, but it is also largely influenced by divine inspiration. If you've been trained Gardnerian, you'd probably be able to pick out the traditional Wiccan elements. If you've been trained through one of the Robert Cochrane lines of the Craft, you'd see that our Traditions are very close cousins. I've had folks with Druidic backgrounds comment openly (and favorably) on the obviously Druidic practices in our rituals. However, there are things that we do that nobody else does. It came to us from the Gods or from the Dragons with whom we work; we have no way of legitimizing it for folks who seek the approval of history books and anthropologists; and we are okay with that.

All of that is to say that my background is Celtic Pagan, non-Wiccan, and eclectic. Our Tradition may be very Celtic in its orientation, but there has always been room for exploration of religious practices outside the Celtic Diaspora. So now, when this self-proclaimed Priestess of Aphrodite drops references to obviously Celtic ritual practice, you'll understand that I am an acknowledged hodge-podge – right in keeping with the broad experience of American Neo-Paganism.

I rather lament that there are very few openly practicing Priestesses in Aphrodisian service. I have very few living role models to guide me on this path. There are a few, and I am managing to find them, but they are constructing their own practice for themselves, much like I am. We are like sisters and brothers to each other as we search for what works for us individually.

So, here I am: a 21st-Century daughter of the Bronze-Age Celts, called into service by the golden-crowned Cytherean, and trying my damnedest to figure it all out.

HISTORICAL BACKGROUND

Aphrodite's worship was likely introduced through Cypress or Cythera, two trade ports who had frequent dealings with Phoenician merchants. Both of these islands claim to be the birthplace of Aphrodite, and the Phoenician travelers probably brought their worship of Ashterah (Astarte, Ishtar) with them. She was the Goddess of Love, of course, and of sexuality, fertility and war.

Among the practices that were associated with these Love Goddesses was the widespread institution of temple prostitution. Though Aphrodite's priestesses served in ways other than merely a sexual capacity, their experience in this area can't be denied. The Temple of Aphrodite at Corinth had 1,000 hierodule (temple priestesses/prostitutes) who came down from agro-Corinth into the town in the evening to ply their art and trade.

Priests and priestesses of love were not quite as

well-known throughout ancient Greece as they were in Sumeria, Canaan and Babylon, though. In the Levantine lands to the east of Helles were many classes and styles of women and women in service of Love. Arguably the oldest written piece of literature, *The Epic of Gilgamesh*, includes at its heart the figure of Shamat. It is she, the sacred prostitute, who civilizes Enkidu, the beast-like wild man who becomes as a brother to the hero Gilgamesh. Shamat brings enlightenment and understanding of man's inherent connection to the Divine. Her union with Enkidu is the union of all that is carnal with all that is spiritual, all that is wild with all that is civilized, all that is past with all that will come.

This is the legacy of the Priestess of Love. We teach the Mysteries of Sacred Union. All opposites, all tensions, all possibilities are represented in that union, and it is our gift to give.

WHY NOW?

The world is in desperate need of all that Aphrodite has to offer. She has been ignored and neglected for millennia. Love is seen as secondary. Joy is a luxury. Celebrate is superfluous. Sex is shameful. This is what the world tells us.

We have rejected our need for true beauty and love, and we have ignored the dark side of these very real, very critical energies. We don't understand our passions or desires, our motivations, and yet they wreak havoc in our lives because we don't have a basic relationship with Love.

It is time. It is finally time for Her Priestesses and Priests to retake their places in the world. It is time for people to acknowledge the layers, dimensions and textures of Love, Beauty and Passion that play such an important role in our lives. It is time that we bit into the apple, taste its sweet flesh, and give thinks to the Kyprian as the golden juice dribbles down our chins!

EXERCISES

1. If you don't do it already, start keeping a journal. Communicating with yourself is the first step to understanding yourself. Set a goal of writing at least three pages in your journal daily. I'm serious. A page-minimum will help keep you focused, and sometimes it'll help you dredge up some of the murkier junk that's been collecting in the corners of your psyche. Fee free to answer questions to this book's exercises in your journal. That absolutely counts as reflective communications.

2. Why did you buy this book? Be honest with yourself. When you made the purchase, what were you hoping to gain? You may have realized that you had a goal when you bought the book, but if not, take stock that you had a purpose already. Though

🌸 APHRODITE'S PRIESTESS

that purpose may change as you read and explore, it is wise to enter any exploration with your eyes open to your own intentions.

3. What is your relationship to Aphrodite (or another Goddess of Love)? Are you call to Priestess/hood? Are you a devoted follower? Are you a curious student?

CHAPTER 2

PRIESTESS OR PROSTITUTE?

WHEN THE LORD, LYING BY HOLY INANNA,

THE SHEPHERD DUMUZI,

WITH MILK AND CREAM THE LAP SHALL HAVE SMOOTHED...

WHEN ON MY VULVA HIS HANDS HE SHALL HAVE LAID,

WHEN LIKE HIS BLACK BOAT, HE SHALL HAVE... IT,

WHEN LIKE HIS NARROW BOAT, HE SHALL HAVE BROUGHT LIFE TO IT,

WHEN ON THE BED HE SHALL HAVE CARESSED ME,

THEN I SHALL CARESS MY LORD, A SWEET FATE I SHALL DECREE FOR HIM,

I SHALL CARESS SHULGI, THE FAITHFUL SHEPHERD,

A SWEET FATE I SHALL DECREE FOR HIM,

I SHALL CARESS HIS LOINS,

THE SHEPHERDSHIP OF ALL THE LANDS, I SHALL DECREE AS HIS FATE.

- INANNA TO DUMUZI (ANCIENT SUMERIAN POETRY)

Nobody who looks seriously at the Aphrodite Priestesshood can deny that temple prostitution was part of the overall organization. The largest known temple to Aphrodite, the one in Corinth, was known for its sacred whores. It is largely because of the widely-known sexual service of the ancient Priestess that many contemporary critics of Aphrodite's new Priestesses will assume them all to be prostitutes. They aren't, and that should be clear up front.

However, it is going to be vital for any who are interested in approaching this Priesstesshood, whether as Priestesses or as supplicants, to have a clear understanding of ancient temple "prostitution" and what it might mean to be a contemporary temple "prostitute." Both are touchy subjects, so it is best to approach this discussion with an open mind.

The subject is touchy enough that you may be wondering why I would start a book about Aphrodite's Priestesshood with a chat about sacred sex when I insist that sex is only one aspect of Her service. The truth is that if we don't clear the air now, we won't be able to talk openly for the rest of the book. Sexual work may be a small percentage of the work that a Priestess does, but it is far from insignificant. Since we may get slapped with the term "prostitute" because of our service, I think we need to be very clear about how the term may or may not apply.

TEMPLE PROSTITUTES IN ANCIENT CORINTH

Most research indicates that the women were primarily *given* to the ancient temple. Daughters were given in devotion to Aphrodite by their families; slaves were offered by their owners. I know it's unfair to judge an ancient culture by contemporary standards, but I can't help being repulsed by this manner of recruitment. Slavery is abhorrent to most of us now, and sexual slavery is sinister and perverse.

Now, I'm not talking about the consensual adult agreements involving "slave and master" that some partners engage in. A real-time, real-world Gohrian culture exists in which women give themselves willingly as slaves to their husbands, as one example. (Gohr is a fictional world created by a fantasy writer, for those unfamiliar with the term.) It's not for me, but I don't necessarily take issue with it. Adults of free-will, in my opinion, have the right to give their will over to another person if they choose.

We have very little evidence about how the women in temples, such as the one in Corinth, felt about their situation. Writers of that time period didn't really consider women's sentiments on their lifestyles, whatever those lifestyles might have looked like. In fact, there is precious little scholarly writing that clearly indicates what any woman's life was like. The women's quarters in the middle and upper class homes were strictly off-limits to men.

It's possible that the temple prostitutes of the ancient world detested and resented their service. It's just as possible, though, that they viewed their service with honor and joy. From the perspective of 2500 years of separation, all any of us can do is speculate about how this Priestesshood was viewed. The only fruitful outcome that is available to us based on this speculation is to envision and create the modern Priestesshood in a way that is positive for its practitioners.

THE CONTEMPORARY PRIESTESSHOOD

It's not really even possible in the free places in the world to re-create the temple as it was in Corinth, and thank Aphrodite for that. The women and men who come to serve Her now come of their own choosing. They come ready to give themselves to Aphrodite in service and in love. They are able to choose the forms their service will take, and they are free to serve themselves and their own needs.

Would it be actual prostitution these days, though? I suppose some might see it that way. Our society is so damned Puritanical, even with our oversexed media images, that women are still slapped with the words "slut" and "whore" and are made to feel ashamed for enjoying their sexuality. You won't find one wearing a large, red "A" on her clothes at the decree of the town, but the brand still sticks. So it is probable that most of the world would view a Priestess who uses the tool of sex as a prostitute. Whether she sees herself that way or not is a whole other issue.

She could, of course, actually be a prostitute, ex-changing money for devotional time in the presence of Aphrodite through the pleasures of sex. This *was* the original scenario. A devotee would come to the temple to honor Aphrodite. The Priestess was the embodiment of Aphrodite, and by lying with the woman, the devotee lies with the Goddess. The money or goods that the devotee gave to the Priestess were votive offerings, of a sort. A way of saying, "Sweet Goddess, you've given me a gift, and I give you one in return." It's no different, in most ways, than giving any other offering to a religious group or entity when you appreciate the work they do. Oh, except that it's technically considered prostitution, which is illegal in the US.

There are two issues to consider about this, as a Priestess who has been called to Aphrodite's service. The first issue deals with the manner in which you serve. Outright sex isn't the only option, after all. In fact, contact with Aphrodite doesn't have to involve any type of sexual contact. Having Aphrodite speak to you, hold your hand or give you a smile are all phenomenal experiences, and all are within the scope of the Priestess's services. The second issue is the exchange that's made between devotee and Priestess. Is it necessary? Does it have to be monetary? Does it even have to be physical?

We're going to explore types of service to Aphrodite later, so I'm not going to go into a full description here. Let's just say that sexual intercourse is just one form of service. There are other physical acts, as well as a world of emotional and spiritual ones, that should grow in the garden of Aphrodite's Priests and Priestesses. If sharing sex with anyone outside of a committed partnership is uncomfortable for you, there's no good reason to push yourself beyond that limit.

Now, as far as "exchange" is concerned, I would think that any reasonable exchange will make the encounter tingle with just the right amount of give and take. After all, it's that give and take that makes all interactions between people pleasurable, whether the interaction is a pleasant conversation or something more intimate.

However, I don't think the exchange needs to be monetary, or any other type of physical gift, in order to be the most beneficial. I suppose, if the devotee and Priestess are strangers, money, jewelry, clothes or other trinkets would be the easiest to accommodate. (However, I have real reservations about the safety of anonymous sex.) I could also assume that in a world of economic realities, in which this type of Priestesshood was welcomed and revered, a woman could expect to earn her livelihood through her ministry, just like most priests and pastors do in our contemporary society. Money and goods would facilitate that sort of living. But, once again, we come back to the legal realities that money can't change hands when sex is involved.

I'm sure that someone could find a loop-hole in the current system by setting up a recognized church, accepting donations, and ministering in whatever ways seem appropriate to the Priestess, the Goddess and Her devotees. What a target, though! It seems dangerous to me on so many levels. The government and police would be looking over the Priestess's shoulder all the time. I'm sure the neighbors wouldn't want THAT type of temple in their neighborhood, making for a hostile environment. A woman with children would likely end up dealing with Child Protective Services. Though some brave souls will undoubtedly pioneer this new frontier, I think that most folks will choose to simply manage the exchange in other ways.

An energetic exchange is most likely. Back in the ol' days, the average devotee wouldn't have been offering to blend their magical energy with that of the Priestess who embodied the Goddess. For one, Greek religion didn't really work that way. For another, this type of exchange takes a more intimate personal connection before the work is to be done. A stranger off the street wouldn't necessarily be the best person with whom to make this exchange. (Again, I really don't recommend picking up strangers for this type of work.)

An exchange of energy would involve both parties (or ALL parties, as the case may be) giving their energy to each other during the interaction, and also taking what is offered from the other. The ancient Priestesses would have done this anyway. They would have been channels for Aphrodite's divine energy and blessings, and they would probably have been giving some of their own energy in the process. One of the reasons for the gift-giving to the Priestess was to acknowledge what she had given and to replenish her. If the devotee can make these acknowledgements and offerings through energy, then money becomes secondary. It might actually be silly to offer money after that type of interaction. Maybe even offensive.

Emotional exchanges, I think, would be the other type of gifting that would sustain a Priestess. My guess is that most Priestesses would begin serving Aphrodite in this way, and many would stay in this realm. If you already truly love the person to whom you are giving Aphrodite's blessings, and you receive that person's love in return, it will feed the power and nature of your work.

This is why Aphrodite was seen as a Goddess who blessed marriages and mother-child relationships. In the give and take between family members who love each other, Aphrodite is already being served, and She is already bestowing Her blessings. The love that flows between lovers is Her gift, and it is given to all who partake of it.

If the Word "Prostitute" Makes You Cringe ...

... we really need to explore the word. "Sticks and stones may break my bones, but words can never hurt me." Right? I think not.

Try explaining to a police officer that you're a "sacred prostitute." I'm pretty sure you'll be spending a night in lock-up with the hookers. Or, go ahead and have a conversation with someone who is curious about Paganism, but is cautious or even concerned because it flies in the face of everything she has been taught. Trot out the word "prostitute," and you'll be able to watch the assumptions forming behind her eyes.

The biggest problems with the word "prostitute" are that actual prostitution is illegal and that people associate the word with the common streetwalker who isn't necessarily freely choosing to engage in her profession. We assume that most women are driven to prostitution as an act of last resort. They trade their bodies for money to fund a nasty drug habit, for instance. We associate them with disease because the best healthcare isn't available to them. We think of them as either being sex addicts or as being emotionally detached from their activities and partners. Enough prostitutes fit this description, so that most of us simply do not have any positive associations with the word (or the profession of) "prostitution." (Of course, I believe that if prostitution were decriminalized, we'd find more respectable and desirable women trading their services, and we could come to a different understanding of prostitution. I also believe that there are enough working girls out there that don't fit the above description to shock mainstream America.)

Looking more deeply into the word, a Priestess of Aphrodite who serves the Goddess by engaging in

actual intercourse still isn't technically a prostitute. Most would choose to use something other
than money for the "exchange" that we've already
discussed. (Honestly, I couldn't advise, in good con-
science, that anyone *should* take money for this sacred service. I've known both women and men who
do charge money as Priestesses of Aphrodite, but
they know that they are outside of the law by doing
this.) However, the idea of emotional detachment is
in opposition to service to the Goddess of Love.
Also, in my opinion, being driven to service through
some outside force (like an addiction), means that
you aren't really serving the Goddess. You're serving yourself. So "prostitution" is an ill-fitting term
for many reasons.

What if "temple prostitute" is the *best* term,
though? I've done a fair amount of consideration of
the other terms, and I simply can't come up with a
better label. Let's explore them together.

SLUT/WHORE

I love the discussion of the titular term from the
book *The Ethical Slut* by Dossie Easton and Catherine A. Liszt. I think they make a fantastic case for
reclaiming the term and wearing it proudly. If a
person enjoys sex and engages in it with multiple
partners and is perfectly pleased by their reasons
for going so, why not reclaim the term? Pagans and
Wiccans have re-assumed the name "Witch" and
have attempted to raise awareness about the true

meaning of the word. The same can be done for "slut" and "whore."

However ... the term doesn't fit for me for two reasons. I know plenty of people who use the phrase "temple whore," and I think they are working admirably to reclaim it. I applaud that effort. However, I dislike the word "whore" for its crudeness. It's a stylistic or linguistic snobbery on my part. It might work for you, and if so, feel free to call yourself (or your representative of the Goddess) by any name that works for you. I just won't be using it in this work.

"Temple slut" just doesn't have the right ring to it. It sounds like a woman who hangs around the temple waiting for the Priestess's leftovers to me. I know, I know! I recognize my linguistic discrimination. I just don't like the phrase.

The second reason, in my mind, for turning away from these words in terms of service to Aphrodite is that they don't imply the "exchange" that is a part of this calling. They imply only a "taking."

PRIESTESS

I am going to use this term quite a bit in the discussions in this book, actually. However, I don't want anyone to mistakenly assume that all Priestesses or Priests of Aphrodite work with sex. In fact, I know plenty of men and women who serve the

Goddess without any sexual contact with other devotees. So "Priestess of Aphrodite" is a term that applies to a group of people with a broad range of skills and specialties, but a "Temple Prostitute" is a subset of the Priesthood.

HIERODULE

This is the Greek term most commonly used to refer to Aphrodite's priestesses. I like the term, for the most part, and I do use it, but I see a couple of small problems with it. The first is that it, technically, means "sacred slave." Now, not all of the women in service were literal slaves as we understand the term, but they did, in a sense, belong to the temple. Some of them paid for the privilege of service, so it's important to understand that, though they might have been considered slaves by ancient Greek standards, they wouldn't' necessarily have been considered such by ours. My first objection, then, is relatively obscure and easily dismissed.

My second objection, though, is that only Grecophiles know the term. Tell someone that you're a hierodule, and you'll quickly be following it up with "That means I'm a Priestess of Love." This can be overcome, I know, but the educational effort involved will have to be very far-reaching.

I use this term to refer to myself, along with Priestess and Qadishtu – all somewhat interchangeably, depending on my audience and how much explanation I feel like offering that day.

QADISHTU/QADESH

This is a term from ancient Canaanite or Babylonian temple prostitution. I actually like this term quite a lot, and I will probably use it synonymously with "temple prostitute." One very real benefit to it is that most English speakers have absolutely no prejudice toward the word. We have the opportunity, then, to build its meaning from the ground up.

However, "qadishtu" does imply a Middle Eastern religious system, as opposed to Greek (or at least, Greek-influenced) religion. Since this book deals with worship of and service to Aphrodite specifically, I hesitate to adopt the term "qadishtu" fully.

CALL GIRL

I like this term based on the connotations, but I don't think "Temple Call Girl" works. It sounds silly. However, I do like that a call girl is generally a classier type of sex worker. She works with a higher-end clientele, and the assumption is that she takes better care of herself than a streetwalker.

COURTESAN

The word "courtesan" evokes images of a classier woman who is in full control of her sexual circumstances, and the term isn't entirely absurd or distasteful to most people. She does what she does, and there is very little stigma attached to her working relationships.

My issue with this word is that a courtesan is such an independent person, that the temple associations would be mostly lost. (And, again, "Temple Courtesan" sounds funny to me.) For all that, though, I could potentially see more temple prostitutes adopting this term to describe what they do.

"Prostitute" It Is

For me, "prostitute" works at least as well as any other term. I encourage readers to explore how these various terms feel to them. Use the terms that feel the most comfortable or that speak to the connotations and the flavors of Priestesshood that you wish to embrace.

De-Criminalizing Prostitution

I've never really understood why prostitution is illegal in most places in the United States. It's a victimless crime when engaged by consenting adults. If it weren't considered a criminal act, we as a society would stand a better chance of ensuring that the women and men offering themselves as prostitutes were in fact consenting and of adult age. Because prostitution happens entirely in the shadows in the US, too man illegal and brutal acts are conjoined with it.

Recently, we have begun to hear more about the sex slave trade that happens here in the US. Women and girls of all ages are abducted, held captive and forced to perform sex acts against their wills. Clearly, this is criminal behavior – and a human rights' violation. But it is one that is perpetuated by our antiquated laws that make sex-for-hire a crime.

If prostitutes and other sex workers were able to practice their trade without fear of arrest, they would be able to gain safe and sanitary working conditions, adequate health care, legal protection against common abuses, and more. Moreover, they would be in a position to control their working conditions in a way that most cannot do right now.

THE LAW

Any priestess who uses sex as one of her professional techniques or tools needs to take the issues of money and the law under serious consideration. They may impact your work more than you know. If you accept gifts from devotees, you may be charged with pandering. Even if you accept nothing from anyone, you'll want to be familiar with the prostitution laws in your state.

Resources

For a complete listing of resources related to prostitution laws and sex workers' rights, see the Appendix.

Exercises

1. Explore the labels/titles addressed int his chapter. Do you have any bog reactions to any of them? Aversions? Resonances? Why do you think this is? Societal conditioning? Personal experiences? Educated consideration? Be honest with yourself and be willing to embrace a titular description for yourself (or someone else) that you hadn't considered before.
2. Evaluate your own stance on the (il)legalities of prostitution. Ruminate for a bit as to whether this affects you, either directly or indirectly. If not now, might it in the future?

For Further Consideration

Qualls-Corbett, Nancy and Marion Woodman. <u>Sacred Prostitute: Eternal Aspect of the Feminine</u>. Inner City Books, 1988.
>A Jungian exploration of the archetype of the temple prostitute. Very compelling reading.

Stubbs, Kenneth Ray, editor. <u>Women of the Light: The New Sacred Prostitute</u>. Access Publishers Network, 1994.

Breton Connelly, Joan. <u>Portrait of a Priestess:
Women and Ritual in Ancient Greece</u>. Princeton
University Press, 2007.
    A well-researched look at the lives, customs
    and expectations of Greek women in divine
    service to the Olympians.

CHAPTER 3

ERECTING THE TEMPLE

OF CYTHEREA, BORN IN CYPRUS, I WILL SING.

SHE GIVES KINDLY GIFTS TO MEN;

SMILES ARE EVER ON HER LOVELY FACE, AND LOVELY IS THE BRIGHTNESS

THAT PLAYS OVER IT.

HAIL, GODDESS, QUEEN OF WELL-BUILT SALAMIS

AND SEA-GIRT CYPRUS; GRANT ME A CHEERFUL SONG.

AND NOW I WILL REMEMBER YOU AND ANOTHER SONG ALSO.

- HOMERIC HYMN TO APHRODITE

The modern temple of Aphrodite may not ever consist of a building, or a complex of buildings, that
house the sacred spaces of Aphrodisian worship
and the Priestesses who minister to Her devotees. It
could, of course, be just such a place, and that
would be fantastic. In fact, worshippers of the
Kyprian may well nurture that fantasy and see it to
fruition with time. The temple, though, will consist
of something more than marble, more than brick
and mortar, for the years of its infancy. The new
temples of Aphrodite will exist only when Her devotees come together to worship and learn; and when
they part, they will each carry a portion of the temple inside themselves.

Indeed, some of these temples are already forming,
though they are far-flung and not terribly commu-
nicative with each other. The Qadishti movement is

one very real aspect of the raising of the temples that is happening. Qadishti are sacred prostitutes from early Middle Eastern practice. Though a qadishtu (feminine) and qadesh (masculine) are not specifically devoted to Aphrodite, there is a great deal of overlap between their work and the work of Aphrodite's Priestesses. It is probably more accurate to say that the role of the qadesh/qadishtu is one of the roles of Priestesshood that will be required in each Golden Temple.

THE GOLDEN TEMPLE

In her book, *Pagan Meditations: The Worlds of Aphrodite, Artemis, and Hestia*, Ginette Paris explores the symbolism and possible meanings of Aphrodite's constant association with gold. With the ideas of longing, perfection, purity and abundance that the precious metal evokes, it is no great wonder that it is so keenly connected to the Kyprian lady.

Sappho wrote, as a part of her invocations of the Muses, "in golden goblets pour richest nectar, thus to delight us," and I see visions of honeyed libations to golden-crowned Aphrodite. Then, I hear in my head the line from the Doors' song "An American Prayer" that calls for "great golden copulations," and I see another form of libation to be poured out in honor of Aphrodite.

From the golden girdle that made Her impossible to

refuse to the golden apple She claimed by the judgment of Paris, Aphrodite is surrounded in imagery of golden hues. I humbly suggest, therefore, that Her temples, as they take shape today, be thought of as golden places of Her worship and study.

THE PRIESTS AND PRIESTESSES

The first role to consider within the temple is that of a Priestess or Priest. What is this person's function? What are his roles? What responsibilities does she hold? What type of training should he experience prior to serving as a Priest? Would there be a need for more than one type of Priestess (or Priest) within the Golden Temple? Let's begin by making a laundry list of the types of duties that will need attendance by Aphrodite's chosen ones.

ACCEPTING GIFTS

Someone will need to be able to receive the offerings that Her devotees wish to make. This could include gifts of material value or physical delight (like money, perfume, fabrics, flowers, wine or chocolates), offerings of poetry and music in Her name, or libations of food and drink. Historically, offerings to the Deities were made at their temples, and the products of those offerings were utilized by the resident Priestesshood (in the cases where the offerings weren't burned, drowned, buried or otherwise made unfit for human use).

Should we assume that this was a gross method of

capitalization by the ancient Priests? Were Aphrodite's early Priestesses gold-diggers in search of sugar daddies to spoil them? Absolutely not! A true and talented Priestess is either in contact with the Goddess (meaning that Aphrodite would be standing just over the shoulder of said Priestess, guiding her words and movements), or she is in possession by the Goddess (so that Aphrodite is "aspecting" or channeling Herself through the face, body and voice of the Priestess) at the time when these gifts and offerings are made. In either case, Aphrodite is the one who receives the gifts of Her devotees. The Priestess is only the physical vessel through which Aphrodite is made manifest.

Does the Priestess get to benefit from the tokens of adoration being given to Aphrodite? Well, that depends. In most cases, I would think so. Unlike many Neo-Pagans, I see nothing inherently wrong with our clergy being paid for their services. In fact, it was through such gift-giving that our predecessors earned a livelihood. The town supported the temple, and vice versa. So, if a woman allows herself to be the face and voice and body of the Goddess to those who would worship Aphrodite, I don't believe it is wrong for her to receive into her own hands, as compensation, the gifts that are freely given. However, she's going to have to be very careful to avoid local prostitution laws, in this case, as she could be raising the suspicion of law enforcement officials.

Could we get into the questionable territory of charlatans who are only looking to turn a profit from the devotion of others? I suppose so. There are nasty people in every walk of life, and the clergy is no exception. I can't imagine, though, that many people would or *could* make a profit through this type of service to Deity. Besides the fact that Aphrodite does terrible things to Priestesses who betray Her (see Chapter 10, "Dark Gold"), one must also contend with the fact that the contemporary Pagan community is not known as a wealthy one. A Priestess of Aphrodite will be more likely to earn spiritual and emotional compensations for her work, rather than ever acquiring much in terms of money or expensive gifts.

MAINTAINING THE TEMPLE SPACE

Another role of the Priestess is to maintain a temple space that is accessible to the devoted worshippers. I can only hope that someday there will be established temple spaces across the globe where men and women can come to pay honor and homage to Aphrodite. There are precious few established Pagan temples of any sort in the world today, let alone ones that house a specific Deity.

The contemporary view on this temple maintenance will probably have to involve the creation of sacred space at regular intervals for those wishing to participate in Aphrodite's rites. In other words, I imagine that most of the Golden Temples will be transitory places – a room bedecked with silks, flowers, icons, cushions and candlelight for a single day or night of Aphrodisian worship at a time. The Priestesses will have to be able to create these places of love and beauty both through physical means (the props and accoutrement already mentioned) as well as through metaphysical means. Those metaphysical means will include the skills of cleansing a space of mundane or profane energies, bringing in a sacred perimeter (like the Witch's circle or the Druid's Grove), and so on. Since this book is not intended as a magical primer, I will not go into the specific methods of completing each of these metaphysical tasks. However, please consult the bibliographic resources for further reading, and seriously consider seeking out a reputable teacher, if you have never done these things before.

As for the physical environment of even a temporary temple, adequate thought needs to be given to comfort, grace and pleasure. This will be a space to which people will come to experience the love and beauty of Aphrodite, and so the space has to reflect that purpose. No matter what the activity within the temple, the Priest or Priestess should take care to ensure that the temperature is appropriate, the room and tools (including bed linens) are clean, the seating or bedding accommodations are comfortable and practical, and that the ambience is conducive to whatever interaction is at hand.

Of course, the more artistic the Priestess is, all the

better, where these duties are concerned. To truly set the mood, an innate understanding of the visual arts is very helpful. Line and color play such a big role in how we perceive absolutely anything that we take in with our eyes. Texture is going to be vital, too, and luxurious and decadent fabrics and surfaces will positively impact the space. Sound and scent each have their place in the scene, as well. The worship of Aphrodite is a sensual experience, and all of the senses must be accommodated in order to most fully achieve your purpose.

Allow me to draw a picture with words of a possible temple scenario:

A tent is erected at a Pagan festival for the purpose of giving attendees the opportunity to hold audience with Aphrodite. The tent is a rather ordinary camping tent, perhaps on the large side so that it can accommodate six to eight sleeping adults almost comfortably. It is not, by its nature, palatial or exotic.

A Priest stands outside the door, though, to welcome worshippers into the temple's sanctuary. Before they enter, the Priest cleanses and blesses each person with khernips, which is saltwater into which a burning brand of incense has been dipped in order to produce a combination of all of the sacred elements. Following this lustration, the Priest holds aside the flap on the temple's door so that the devotee may enter.

Inside, the tent is adorned with lengths of crimson silk that hang from the apex of the structure to its corners. The fabric falls in watery folds to the floor where a carpet of scarlet and gold is spread in an oval. At the side and back of the temple is a chair upon which a woman sits. She is draped in red silks threaded with gold. Her dark blond hair cascades down her exposed shoulders.

The petitioner is offered a seat upon a velvet cushion before the Priestess. Other cushions, in rich brocades and jewel-toned satins, litter the edges of the space. A water-filled crystal bowl sits atop an ebony-dark altar strewn with rose petals. A white candle flickers in a golden taper-holder. Incense gently wafts from the altar, filling the space with the scents of amber and myrrh. Soft music exudes from a hidden source so that the faint sounds of drums echo the pounding of the petitioner's heart. Gentle chimes in the music send chills of excitement through the temple and its occupants.

Beats the heck out of a sleeping bag on the living room floor, incandescent overhead lights and a barking dog, doesn't it?

INVOKING THE GODDESS

In my particular Pagan tradition, we understand the word "invocation" to be synonymous with "possession" or "channeling." When a Priestess invokes a Goddess, she is allowing her entire body to be filled up with that Deity. Whatever use the Deity has for the body is generally allowed, depending on the experience and limitations of the Priestess. This is a skill that we practice in controlled, supervised settings until we have demonstrated the ability to reclaim our own bodies after the experience without adverse reactions. It is not something that we do lightly or that we allow newbies to attempt without help.

All of those warnings having been said, a functioning Golden Temple should have at least one Priestess or Priest who can adequately hold and release the energy of Deity in this way. Preferably, the temple would have both a Priest and a Priestess so that, together, they can perform the Sacred Marriage (see Chapter 9).

The intermediate step to possession is what I know as "contact." During contact, the Deity is close (sometimes, extraordinarily close) to the Priestess, but the mortal still retains full control of her body and mind. In this state, she can hear, see, smell and feel the Goddess. This is a much safer practice for beginners, and it can accomplish similar goals.

Being able to achieve at least a contact means that Aphrodite will be fully present for any workings in Her honor. It means that She will actually be offering Her blessings, with the Priestess acting as an intermediary to convey those blessings.

However, if the Priestess is able to achieve a full possession with the Goddess, then Aphrodite will be present incarnate for the work done in Her temple. She can literally reach out and touch the celebrants with a warm, soft hand, if She chooses.

COUNSELING AND HEALING

I believe that one of the key roles of a Priestess of Aphrodite is to help heal the hurts of the people around her. Sometimes they are aware of the capacity in which you heal them, sometimes they are oblivious. It really doesn't matter. The fact is that Her Priests and Priestesses are called, very frequently, to help others work through and grow beyond their pain.

The tools available to us for this role are innumerable. Traditional counseling styles can work here. Ritual drama and role-playing are not to be overlooked. Sexual and sensual intimacies are very effective – and a whole lot of fun.

At its essence, though, the force at work is that of Love. With the Priestess acting as a conduit for the love of Aphrodite, anything is possible. Raw and bloody emotional wounds can be wiped clean. Festering insecurities can finally be abandoned and forgotten. Broken bonds can be re-forged. A broken person can be made whole.

Some Priests and Priestesses will be naturally talented in this area. Surely, most everyone who is called to this service will have one or more methods of loving others already at their disposal. However gifted a person may already be in this arena, a little extra training and practice will refine and deepen those skills. Counseling classes at a local college or workshops on Pagan counseling at festivals might be in order, for example. One of the skills that any non-professional counselor should have is the ability to recognize when a person needs more help than you can give.

As for ritual drama, role-playing and sex work, we'll talk more about how these tools are a part of the liturgy of Aphrodite in the next chapter. One idea to bear in mind where these skills are concerned: practice makes perfect, and the practice is a whole lot of fun!

QADISHTI

I've mentioned the qadishti before in connection with sexual service. The qadishti are the temple prostitutes who specialize in the sexual work of the Golden Temples. Not all of those called to Aphrodite's service will honor Her in this way, but many will. Indeed, in our prudish society that fears sexuality (and doubly fears a woman in control of her sexuality), I imagine that many *will* be called to serve this way who refuse based on their own fear.

Physical love is the gift of the qadishtu. Not just

sexual intercourse, mind you. Touching, kissing, massaging, holding – these are all aspects of physical love. As humans, we have a deep need to be touched. Too many people are shunned and neglected – they are unwanted by the world, and nobody reaches out to them.

Within the sacred bedchamber, all are lovely. All are beloved. All are loved. That is the gift of a qadesh. That is the blessing of the qadishtu. Qadishti offer the touch of Aphrodite in the lives of those around them.

TEMPLE DOG

The Hebrews called the Canaanite priests and priestesses "dogs" as an insult, but it was a term that the qadishti spun to their own liking. They used it to mean one who is loyal and protective of the temple. The kelevh (temple dog) is usually a male priest who acts in a ministerial/managerial function. He sees to the flow of temple work, and it is his primary duty to protect those in his care. Modern priestess of sacred sexuality need to consider their own physical safety, and working in tandem with a kelevh (or a Temple Guard, if you prefer the term), is a logical choice.

DEVOTEES

The Priests and Priestesses are not the only members of the temple, of course, so we should spend some time discussing the characteristics and roles of those who come to worship Kypris.

In a strictly literal sense, all of the members of the Golden Temple are devotees of Aphrodite. They are all devoted to worshiping Her. Each one, Priests and Priestesses included, will receive Her blessings at the hands of the others with whom they worship. No single member of a temple will have all of the keys to unlocking the golden gates of Her most secret gardens, and so all will continue to learn and grow as students of the Goddess.

The fact remains, though, that some folks are called to serve Her more consistently or more specifically. These Priests and Priestess are no more important in the workings of the temple, and they are certainly no more glamorous or enviable. The title is a designation of calling. It is a vocation. It is not a rank or an indicator of power over others.

So those who come bearing gifts and seeking blessing, those who come to stand in the presence of Deity, those who come to be healed within Her halls, those are the Devoted. They hear Aphrodite's call, or want to hear it. They feel Her touch, and they yearn for it. They represent everyman, and they are too diverse and complex to summarize.

Together, these are the members of the Golden Temple. They are of every (legally consenting) age, of every nationality, of every background, of every occupation. They come together in love and in trust to touch and be touched by the grace of the golden-crowned, golden-shod Queen of Heaven and of Earth.

EXERCISES

1.   Are there aspects of service described in this chapter that hold particular appeal to you? What are they? Why do you feel drawn to them?
2.   Are there duties here that you feel like you could do (and maybe do well), but to which you feel an aversion? Explore this resistance.
Can you identify any aspects of service to Aphrodite that may be missing from this list? In what other ways might you honor Her as a Priestess?

FOR FURTHER CONSIDERATION

Gardner, Kevin. The Wiccan Minister's Manual. Author House

Gardner, Kevin. A Handbook for Wiccan Clergy. Author House.

> These books have a distinctly Wiccan flavor, which isn't entirely applicable to our work, but they are excellent resources for those called to leadership aspects of this service.

CHAPTER 4
LITURGY OF GRACE

I TURN THE MALE TO THE
FEMALE. I AM SHE WHO
ADORNETH THE MALE FOR THE
FEMALE; I AM SHE WHO
ADORNETH THE FEMALE
FOR THE MALE.
- INANNA (ATTRIBUTED)

When it comes to rituals that can be devised to honor Aphrodite, the possibilities are limitless. I think it is possible to write an entire book of liturgy for worshipping and working with Her. Though I might like to take on that task at some point, I'm going to focus on some highlights for the scope of this current work.

FORM AND FORMAT

The type of ritual structure one uses really depends on the specific Tradition that one follows. Wiccans could certainly cast a circle and call the quarters. Druid-based Pagan groups, like mine, can call the ancient Grove and the three Realms of Sky, Land and Sea. The key, I think, is in establishing the space as sacred, however that works for you.

In the absence of a preferred working format, you

can use a Greek system. According to Walter Burkert in his book *Greek Religion*, sacred sites like temples and groves remained sacred. Unlike the common Wiccan/Neo-Pagan practice that essentially involves recreating sacred space at the beginning of every ritual, the ancient Greeks believed that the space stayed put.

Of course, they had dedicated temples and groves that weren't used for mundane activities in any way. They were ritually cleansed at regular intervals (yearly or seasonally), but they didn't attract as much muck that needed to be cleared out as the Wiccan's living room that doubles as a ritual site.

Burkert explains that prior to beginning a ritual at a sacred site outside of a temple area, such as a grove of trees, representatives of the same basic elements used by Neo-Pagans would walk around the ritual site carrying symbols of the elements. This process really didn't resemble casting a circle or calling the quarters, though. In fact, the Greeks viewed the elements slightly differently than most Neo-Pagans have been taught to view them. For example, certain ritual participants who walked the boundaries of the sacred space might carry a bowl, a container of water, a basket, fire and a bough (sacred tree limb). These items were certainly carried during the procession to the festival that preceded high celebrations.

Khernips was also used as a cleansing preparation

in ritual spaces. Khernips is made by sanctifying (through word and symbol) salt, water, flame and incense. The salt is then mixed with the water, the incense is lit so that it is flaming and smoking, and then the lit incense is extinguished in the saltwater. This is a ritual combination of earth, water, fire and air, and it is an extraordinarily purifying solution that can be used to cleanse the space.

Whether in the grove or the temple, a quick ritual bath, or lustration, was in order. Before entering the sacred space, or shortly after entering but before the rites began, each participant would be sprinkled with water for purification. They would also pour water over their hands.

There are a few other trademarks of Greek ritual. I would recommend that anyone interested in Hellenismos or Greek Reconstructionism consult one or more of the texts in this book's bibliography.

Though I would agree that authentic Greek ritual forms could be desirable when working with a Greek deity, I'm not really a Greek Reconstructionist, myself. I work with Aphrodite in a blended ritual format that borrows from both Greek and Celtic structures. For that reason, I'm going to offer some suggestions for a blend – Greek-Wiccan. I figure that combination will be the most useful for the widest range of interested folks. After all, "Wiccan" is practically the universal language of Pagan ritual. With the Pagan "Rosetta Stone," folks can easily translate Wiccan ritual forms into whatever suits their particular tastes.

BASIC RITUAL FORMAT (BLENDED)

The basic format that I am suggesting is synthesized from several sources. My own experience in ritual, Jennifer Reif's work *Demeter*, and Walter Burkert's research are the three main ingredients. This is only a suggestion, and only one way (of a thousand) that these rituals might be approached. Use, lose or abuse this material as you see fit.

A general outline, applicable to nearly any ritual purpose, might be as follows:

> Call to ritual
> Cleansing the participants
> Establishing sacred space
> Welcome
> Inviting Aphrodite and Her retinue
> Offering (usually sacred touch, a sacrifice of
>   some sort or a ritual drama)
> Libation
> Releasing of everything called to the space

CALL TO RITUAL

A herald calls the members of the ritual to the space. This denotes the change from mundane to sacred. It is a marking of the difference between everything that happens outside of the temple and all that happens within it. In the case of a ritual that a particular group might deem as a Mystery, the herald would administer a vow of silence here, insuring that participants not speak casually about those things that have experienced as sacred. Since the Cults dedicated to each Olympian were Mystery schools, this could be appropriate for nearly any ritual.

CLEANSING THE PARTICIPANTS

Everyone brings profane energies with them. The lustration is a ritual cleansing of the participants so that they are clean in a spiritual sense, making them free to enter the temple and engage in ritual. The person who fulfills this duty in ritual, we will call the Hydranos Priestess, or the Hydrophorous.

The cleansing itself might take a couple of forms. One common way to accomplish this in a modern Wiccan ritual is to sprinkle the celebrant with droplets of water. In the ancient Greek context, it was more common to pour water over the celebrant's hands, and then allow him to wash his face.

ESTABLISHING SACRED SPACE

This is the point at which the temple is erected, in our case. Traditionally, it was walking the bounds of the space with the elemental items to mark the space as sacred.

We will cast the circle and call the quarters, with their many protections. To bring the Greek flavor to the ritual, we can use the same or similar items to denote the elements.

Welcome to Ritual

The purpose of the welcome is twofold. First, it establishes the purpose of the ritual. A speaker would announce the intent behind the ritual within the confines of magical space to be certain that the participants understand, and the Gods are made fully aware of the work that is to be done on Their behalf.

The second purpose for the welcome is to reinforce the vow and the group's intention to continue in the rite.

Inviting Aphrodite and Her Retinue

It is at this point that the Graces and Oreads are called to attend, that the characters of the Sacred Drama are invoked by their "actors," and that Aphrodite is brought into manifestation through the body of the Priestess.

You may use ancient poetry for this purpose, or you may write your own words. However, a basic format for prayer exists in Greek religion, and it also works for properly calling on the Gods.

PRAYER (AND EVOCATION/INVOCATION)

Greeting or salutation ("Hail, Aphrodite!")
Naming ("Aphrodite Ourania and Aphrodite Pandemos, Queen of Heaven and Queen of Earth. Aphrodite Acidalia, rising from the bath.") Either a list of epithets or an explanation of the names (which also reveals something about the character of the Deity being called) is equally appropriate. Generally, it's good to include a catch-all like, "Aphrodite, by whatever ever name You prefer."
Recognizing the Deity's favorite places ("from Cypress, from Cytherea," etc.) Again, a universal phrase like, "or from those secret places You most enjoy," is a common addition.
Listing past favors, on both sides ("You've come to me when I called You and have wiped away my tears of grief, replacing them with joy and laughter. I have been Your faithful servant, bringing Your love and beauty into the world around me.") This establishes the connection between the Deity and the supplicant.
Request ("Be with us now, Aphrodite, and bless us with Your presence. Guide us as we explore Your Mysteries. Allow us to come close to You and receive Your blessings.")
Vow ("We will honor You and give You liba-

tions of sweetest fruit. We will carry Your love into the world.") Greek religion is set up as a give and take between mortals and immortals. They work for each other, and the bond is very real. These votive offerings strengthen those ties. The vow itself can exist of nearly any action or physical gift. Just be sure to follow through on it!

Regarding the order in which to call, I prefer to call the Oreads (woodland nymphs) first, then the Graces (akin to the Muses, they are lesser Goddesses of Mirth, Splendor and Good Cheer), followed by the mortal characters of the drama, any Deific participants in the drama, and, finally, Aphrodite.

OFFERING

This part of the ritual is only limited by imagination. We could probably characterize nearly anything that happens here as either sacrifice, ritual drama, or sacred touch, though.

SACRIFICE

The Greek practice of sacrifice usually did involve ritual animal slaughter. However, the entire animal was utilized for the benefit of the Gods and the community. The parts that could be eaten were cooked and used as the staple of the feast. The blood and intestines were used as tools of divination and prophecy. The remainder was burnt as the food of he Gods.

I'm not going to make any recommendations one way or the other about ritual animal sacrifice for religious practices. Frankly, when handled the way it was by the Greeks, it is a sane and reasonable practice. Anyone who grew up on a farm and was involved in the slaughter of animals can probably see the sense in that. However, it isn't really a practice for which most contemporary Pagans have the appropriate sensibilities (or opportunity). If we lived closer to the land, perhaps it would make more sense and be more of a true sacrifice. We don't, though, and the practice is largely lost on us.

From a purely Aphrodisian perspective, there is reason to believe that an animal sacrifice wouldn't be appropriate anyway. Several writers, Homer included, have indicated that Aphrodite was repulsed by bloodshed and burnt animal sacrifice in Her name. A much more common offering was that of incense, and there are several descriptions of incense altars in apple groves for the worship of Aphrodite.

Releasing doves would be a beautiful and inspirational gesture, as well. Another sacrifice, one that was often made by common prostitutes, was the giving up of their mirrors or cosmetics. Perfume, jewelry, chocolates, wine and honey also make lovely sacrifices and offerings to the Kyprian.

DRAMA

Ritual drama is most explicitly related to Dionysos, but it can be performed in honor of other Deities as well. In fact, ritual drama and role-playing are both incredibly powerful ways to experience the Mysteries. They allow their participants to "go behind the mask" and act, move, think and feel in ways that might otherwise be impossible for them. They also allow catharsis (a cleansing of the emotions and spirit) for the audience.

A good friend of mine, and a leader in the Qadishti Movement, uses role-playing extensively in his work with sacred sexuality. Borrowing from the BDSM scene, he applied the principles of "putting on a character" and engaging in consensual scenes with his wife. They primarily invoke Deities from the Mediterranean, Middle Eastern and Mesopotamian pantheons in order to experience the force of the interactions between these entities. (They don't mix pantheons in a single engagement, in case that point isn't immediately clear.) Not only is this work incredibly enlightening, it is excruciatingly hot.

I would like to make a note here that novice practitioners shouldn't go around inviting Deities to possess their bodies. I have been taught, and I believe to be true, that one needs to be skilled enough to bring in, hold and release he Deity in the presence of more skilled Priests or Priestesses until these skills are proven. The role-play we're discussing doesn't have to involve what we might call "possession." It is also extremely effective with what we've already discussed as "contact."

A few practices that the BDSM lifestyle incorporates that would be wise for role-players in sacred space to adopt include the use of negotiations and safe-words. Negotiate the scene to be played beforehand, and don't go beyond the limits of that scene. Also, determine a safe-word beforehand that any participant may use to bring the scene to an immediate halt. Both negotiating and using safe-words are mechanisms that insure the physical and emotional safety of all concerned.

SACRED TOUCH

The "Sacred Touch Ceremony" is a specific ritual practice that was developed by my friend and mentor, Michael A. Manor, in his work with the Qadishti Movement. I offer a very basic description here because I feel like this is an integral ceremony for the Aphrodite priestesshood. Elements of this ceremony would work well for any practitioners of sacred sex.

Essentially, the Ceremony of Sacred Touch has 3 parts: define your limits, give pleasure, receive pleasure. Simple, eh?

The participants sit in a circle around a bed or pallet on the floor. The first person moves to the center and is given as much time as she needs to describe the limits of the experience she wishes to receive. She may include a list of "don'ts" ("Don' touch me below the belt. Don't tickle me. Don't stick your tongue in my ear because it weirds me out."); and she is encouraged to give a list of "dos" ("Do growl and bite my neck. It makes my toes curl. Do stroke my hair.")

Once this limit-setting has taken place, she either sits, stands or lies down, and the people around her give her loving touch within the parameters that she set. Many hands, lips, teeth, tongues and voices move as one to pour out love and pleasure to this one person.

A person's turn in the center ends either when the group stops giving (usually by a beautiful and unconscious consensus that the work is complete) or when the person in the middle speaks the group's safe-word.

The beauty of this ceremony is that everyone gets a turn receiving the pleasurable touch that he needs, and everyone experiences the joy of giving love and pleasure to others. The interaction can be playful and light, or intensely erotic, and that tone is likely to shift from one person to the next, depending on what is needed.

Though the Sacred Touch Ceremony is a specific practice, I'm also using "sacred touch" to indicate any number of loving experiences of contact, touch and even sex that might occur as a part of the primary working of an Aphrodite ritual. The Great Rite, or Heiros Gamos, is one example of sacred touch, as is the ceremony of touch described above.

LIBATION

The libation is the consummation of the work. It seals the working that has been done, offers a final thanks to the Gods and Beings who were present, and it helps to ground the ritual participants so that they can come back to consensus reality.

The libation for Wiccan rituals is usually called "Cakes and Ale." It can consist of any food and drink that suits the ritual and the Deities being served. For a "Greek touch," be sure to offer a healthy libation to the Gods themselves by pouring the food and drink to the ground or into a libation bowl.

RELEASE OF THE SACRED

Say farewell and give thanks to any entities and spaces that you called forward. This is both polite and safe. Expecting Deities and beings to hang around is rude, and leaving energy portals open welcomes trouble from the other side. So, say goodbye and close and lock the doors after your visit.

BITS OF GREEK LITURGY

Finding scholarly documentation for specific ritual and spiritual practices among the ancient and classical Greeks is somewhat difficult. Finding information about rituals and offerings to Aphrodite is nearly impossible.

In fact, the only clear and explicit indication that we are given from ancient texts regarding the worship of Aphrodite was written in Empedocles' *Porphyrius de abstinentia*.

> "They had no god Ares nor Kudoimos,
> nor king Zeus nor Kronos nor Poseidon,
> but Kupris as queen.
> Her did they propitiate with holy images,
> with images of living creatures,
> with perfumes of varied fragrance
> and with sacrifice of pure myrrh and sweet-scented frankincense,
> casting to the ground libations of golden honey.
> Their altar was not steeped in the pure blood of bulls
> but rather was this the greatest abomination among men,
> to tear out the life from the goodly limbs and eat them."

This passage gives us lots of valuable information. Myrrh and frankincense are clearly sacred to Aphrodite, as is honey. Also, animal sacrifices are not appropriate when honoring Her. Many historians have indicated that doves were sacrificed to Her. Rather, they were probably released to their freedom, and the sacrifice didn't need to involve bloodshed.

Jennifer Reif, a modern writer from Southern California and a follower of a Greek tradition, wrote a very interesting book regarding the cycles of Demeter. In her book, she includes rituals for these festivals and Mystery rites. In the Greater Mystery rite, Aphrodite has a role. There is an altar in Her honor, and Reif describes its set-up.

The Aphrodite altar that Reif describes is arranged on a table against a wall. She suggests covering it in a blue cloth and placing an icon or image of Aphrodite on it. She also recommends a large chalice filled with water and decorated with trailing, blue ribbons. There should be a candle there to be lit for Her, and roses to be given as an offering to Her. Furthermore, she says that seashells, flowers and images of doves are all appropriate.

Of course, there is nothing extraordinarily scholarly about these suggestions. Aphrodite is a Goddess of the sea, and all of the images and tokens are oceanic. I am sure that these choices are intuitive; and, although they are certainly valid, they

don't come out of research of ancient work. Therefore, we continue to be free to make our own symbolic associations as suit us.

Another modern writer, who published under the
name Epaphroditus, wrote a ritual drama in honor
of Aphrodite as Philotes. The name Philotes means
Love. Although this particular writer suggests
Philotes is a daughter of Aphrodite, which may certainly be true, the classical poet Empedocles saw
Her as the same being.

In this drama, Epaphroditus shares the four sacraments of Love. The first is the Sacrament of the Self
– knowing and loving one's self as God and Goddess. This was emphasized through the use of a
mirror. The others are the Sacraments of Sight,
Skin and Sex. Epaphroditus also includes as a part
of the work, the "Sign and Seal" of the devotees of
Philotes: "May Love's embrace encircle thee. I welcome Love; so let it be!"

Although this is clearly a modern work and a contemporary understanding of the ancient beliefs, I
find a very strong personal connection and reso-
nance to it. My own intuition says that there is a
great deal of Truth and mystery involved in this ritual.

Finally, there is some meager information available
regarding the celebrations and festivals in honor of
Aphrodite. Several sources indicate that the 4th day

of every month (counted in the old lunar method) is sacred to Aphrodite. Indeed, April 4th is often indicated as Her birthday, and the month's name is based on one of Aphrodite's epithets. The Full Moon in April is considered sacred to Her. Furthermore, the first two days of April were honored with the "Festival of Peace." This festival celebrated the way in which the power of love overcomes the physical power of Ares – April overtakes March (Mars). The old saying "Amor Vincit Omnia" (Love Conquers All) may be a vestige of this festival's premise.

The month of Hekatombaion, which is roughly from mid-July to mid-August in the modern calendar, began the Athenian year. The Aphrodisia took place on the 4th of this month. The Aphrodisia was the bathing festival of Aphrodite Pandemos and Peitho (Persuasion), Her Helper. Some sources also list Peitho as one of Aphrodite's daughters. According to one source, the festival begins when the temple is purified with dove's blood and the altar is anointed. The activity of the festival mainly includes the washing of sacred images.

Finally, there is some indication that Aphrodite may have had Her hand in some of the activities for the festival of Gamelia. The month of Gamelion, "Month of Marriage," is very popular for weddings. Gamelia is at the end of the month, and it is a celebration of the sacred marriage of Zeus and Hera. One writer suggests using intuition to discover some of the secrets behind this festival. My intuition tells me that the Goddess who blesses marriage would definitely have been invoked, indeed would have been a central figure, in such a celebration.

FODDER FOR RITUAL

To find inspiration for creating rites and rituals, we might look to a number of sources. My favorites, though, and the ones that are the most meaningful in my experience, involve taking a look at the mythologies and legends of the Deities with which we work. Whether we are re-enacting a story or examining the underlying concepts, the old stories are full of lessons for contemporary society.

Glimpses of Aphrodite are shared in Homer's *Iliad* and in his hymns, in the histories of Apollodorus and Hesiod, and in the lyric poetry of Sappho. Her stories are captured in sculpture and pottery. We can interpret so much from these sources, and we can extrapolate so much more for ourselves. Her lovers and children, Her relationships with other Goddesses, Her followers, and Her symbols all provide us with rich sources of insight, if we take the time to look and think and feel.

LOVERS

As a Goddess of Love, Aphrodite's romantic relationships are of a great deal of importance. They

show us the archetypes of various human relationships, and show us where and how we can improve
our encounters with our loved ones. Furthermore,
Her romantic interludes often illustrate types of relationships that we would be wise to avoid. Finally,
in a historical sense, they provide us with an understanding of some of the political alliances and
cultural norms that were prevalent in ancient and
classical Greece.

Aphrodite was married to Hephaestus, the lame
son of Hera. He was club-footed and sooty, due to
his role as forge-keeper. He was a craftsman of the
finest degree, and he showered Her with gifts, although many legends say She had nothing but dis-
dain for him.

She was given to him as bride when Zeus realized
how the other Gods were fighting for Her. To avoid
trouble, and to provide Her with a stable home life,
he forced Her to marry the loving, if not suave,
forge master. Hephaestus showered Her with gifts
of wrought gold and precious jewels, despite Her
infidelity.

Actually, very few, if any of the Gods of Olympus
were faithful to their spouses by modern standards. Aphrodite is criticized for Her affairs with
Gods and mortals, but little mention is usually
made about the various other brides and lovers
with whom Hephaestus is credited. Both the Goddess Athena and the Grace Euphrosyne are also

said to be his wives, and they were undoubtedly his lovers.

Athena, specifically, is linked with Hephaestus due to their similar associations with the forge and smithcraft. One might even surmise that some of the animosity between Athena and Aphrodite could be attributed to the fact that Aphrodite was forced to marry Hephaestus and Athena chose to love him willingly. Perhaps Aphrodite was jealous of the bond shared between the two, while Athena could have been resentful of Aphrodite's sometimes inconsiderate attitude to the God She (Athena) so loved and admired.

Nevertheless, it has always been my contention that Aphrodite did love and admire Her husband. I once lead a full moon ritual based on the fact that the Lady sees all beauty, wherever it may lie. Hephaestus had great skill in working with precious stones and metals, and he made beautiful gifts for both his wife and others. Aphrodite is capable of seeing and appreciating the beauty inside him. She is not so superficial a Goddess, as modern thought would have us believe, that She was incapable of loving a man whose beauty did not lie on the surface.

Among the many treasures that Hephaestus made, one of the most famous is Her *cestas*. This was a golden girdle that made both men and Gods helpless to resist its wearer. Needless to say, Aphrodite made good use of this wonderful device – as if She needed it!

Ares was probably Her most famous lover among the Gods. In *The Odyssey*, a singer tells how Aphrodite and Ares were caught in Her husband's bed by Helios. Hephaestus made an unbreakable net to catch them and brought them before the other Olympians. He demanded the adulterer's damage – the return of his gifts of courtship. Poseidon offered to cover this payment if Ares defaulted in his vow. Aphrodite went to Cypress to be bathed by the Graces. Ares went to Thrace to do who knows what. After the incident, Apollo asked Hermes how he would feel at such indignity. Hermes said he would suffer three time the bonds if only he could bed Aphrodite.

Aphrodite's relationship with Ares eternally links love and war. Great passion frequently leads to passionate and angry words, and eventually to battle. Furthermore, there are specific acts, such as rape, that are a singular result of the union between sex and aggression. Aphrodite's on-going affair with the God of War shows us much of Aphrodite's darker, more dangerous, and more volatile side (which we'll explore in greater detail in Ch.10).

Adonis is arguably Her most well-known mortal lover. In the version of the story recorded by Apollodorus in his work *Library and Epitome*, Aphrodite entrusted Persephone with the infant Adonis, but

Persephone became enamored of the beautiful child and tried to keep him. Zeus decreed that Adonis would divide his year in thirds. One third of the year, he would spend alone. One third he would spend with Persephone. The other third was to be spent with Aphrodite. Because of the love he bore to Aphrodite, he chose to spend his own third with Her as well.

CHILDREN

The Goddess of Love had a great deal of love to share with Her children. Knowing that Her roots lie with the fertility and mother Goddesses of the Fertile Crescent, it is no wonder that She is the mother of so many figures in Greek mythology.

Her children were fathered by Her many lovers, although there is no story that indicates that She bore children to Hephaestus. The children are frequently the physical representations of the union of Aphrodite's traits with those of Her lovers.

By Ares, She bore a daughter, Harmonia. Hephaestus made a necklace that Harmonia wore on Her wedding day. Some versions of the story say that he made it for Her specifically. Others say that he made it for Aphrodite, and She chose to give it to Her daughter.

The fact that Harmonia is Ares' daughter by Aphrodite shows us that harmony can, in fact, be the result of war-like and aggressive confrontations. Sometimes the anger and destruction of Ares are exactly what is needed to clear the air to make way for harmony.

Aphrodite bore two other children to Ares, as well. They were Phobos and Deimos, Fear and Panic, "the shield-piercer." Hesiod describes them as "terrible Gods who drive in disorder the close ranks of men in numbing war." I know one servant of Aphrodite who reminds those with whom he works that Phobos and Deimos are not only their father's children. Fear and panic are common in love, as well, and they are worth embracing and understanding as such.

Finally, she bore Anteros to Ares. Anteros punished those who failed to return the love of others. All of these were passed off as the children of Hephaestus.

By Dionysos, She gave birth to Priapus, a grotesque fertility God who was associated with human lust. She also bore Hymen, who was the God of marriage. Some sources also account the Graces as the children of Aphrodite and Dionysos. In one respect, this makes complete sense. However, very little documentation exists to support this claim. Furthermore, the Graces attended the Lady at Her birth, making it somewhat difficult for them to be Her children.

By Hermes, She gave birth to Hermaphroditus, who was welded with a nymph into a body with both sexes. I see one of the lessons here to be that traditionally masculine roles and traditionally feminine roles can be blended in the body of one person. In fact, they frequently are. Hermaphroditus is a reminder to us all that we both hold the male and the female principles within ourselves.

By Zeus, who is sometimes accounted as Her father, She gave birth to Eros, who is the creator of sensual love. Eros is usually depicted as a winged infant with a quiver full of arrows (love darts) that never miss their marks. These arrows affect both Gods and men. Interestingly, Eros (Love) was conceived on the day of Aphrodite's birth, according to Plato. He is stronger than Ares because Ares was caught by Love – of Aphrodite. Plato explains that, "The captor is stronger than the caught, and as he controls what is braver than any other, he must be the bravest of all."

By Anchises, a Trojan shepherd, she bore Aeneas, who became the founder of Italy, and is thereby considered to be the mythical ancestor of the Roman people. Aphrodite, or Venus, is the namesake of the city of Venice where a golden ring is thrown into the sea every year at a festival in Her honor.

FEMALE RELATIONSHIPS

Her relationships with other Goddesses have also

been recorded with some care. They, too, give us insight into the nature of the most adored Lady. To speak truth, She wasn't entirely adored by the other Goddesses.

Her tension with Athena has already been mentioned. Despite this long-standing tension, there are allusions in literature to the fact that They did sometimes work together toward the same goals. Nevertheless, there was a sense of competition and struggle between Them, at least during the Trojan War.

Homer, in his 5th hymn, mentions the three Goddesses whom Aphrodite cannot ensnare. The first, of course, is Athena. The reason he gives for Aphrodite's inability to persuade Athena is that Athena loves war and "preparing famous crafts." Furthermore, she "has no pleasure in the deeds of Aphrodite."

The second Goddess is Artemis, because she loves hunting, archery, the lyre, dancing, thrilling cries, shady woods and cities of men. Artemis is more "untamed" than Aphrodite. Truly, both Artemis and Athena may be considered "tom-boys" by modern standards, and Aphrodite is certainly more of a "girly-girl." Essentially, Athena and Artemis are simply not interested in Aphrodite, nor She in Them. They share very little in common other than the fact that all are described as beautiful.

The final Goddess who Aphrodite could not ensnare was Hestia. The reason Homer gives for this is the fact that Hestia wanted to remain a maiden all Her days. She stubbornly refused to wed either Poseidon or Apollo. Zeus gave Her a place of honor in every house and temple – the hearth. However, she refused the gifts of love that Aphrodite bestows, and so She is outside of Aphrodite's influence.

RETINUE

Aphrodite, as all Goddess do, has a contingent of followers, both mortal and immortal. She was adored by demi-Deities, and several chose to be in Her company as much as possible. Two groups, especially, have strong associations with Her.

The Graces were a group of three sisters who had a function similar to that of the Muses. They are generally said to be the daughters of Zeus and Eurynome, daughter of Ocean. The three "fair-cheeked Charities" are named Aglaea, Euphrosyne and Thalia. Hesiod says of Them that from Their eyes "as they glanced flowed love that unnerves the limbs; and beautiful is their glance beneath their brows."

Finding information on the Graces is considerably more difficult than one would think. For this reason, much of the information included here has been "reconstructed" through meditation, divination and pathworking. It will not be supported in classical or scholarly texts, but it is nevertheless true (for me).

The Graces are three queens of change. They assist in removing walls and blockages that hinder beauty and love and happiness. This happens in both a physical sense and in a spiritual one. Although They generally present Their gifts in moderation, They sometimes find joy in excess, which can be a little dangerous.

Aglaea, whose name means Splendor, is associated with fiery passion. She frequently brings competition regarding physical beauty. This can be as harmless as the typical beauty pageant. However, it can also be destructive when it leads to extreme vanity and the competition that brings animosity between friends. She bestows Her traits as She deems, but she also rewards those who work for Her gifts. Awe-inspiring beauty and charm are Hers to give.

Euphrosyne, Mirth, is a lady of the Air. Giggles and jokes are definitely Hers. There is some indication that Libra, the cardinal sign of Air, is associated with Her. She is intelligent and cunning, and finds humor and play wherever She can. However, She is also capable of extremely focused and purposeful attention. This shift may be misinterpreted by many who do not understand that mirth is still present.

Thalia, Good Cheer, is the youngest of the Graces. She is earthier and more consistently blithe than Euphrosyne. As the youngest, She is the most energetic. She also has an unexpected nature. Despite Her "earthiness," which usually serves to ground a figure and keep them more fully planted, She represents some aspects of illusion and trance. In fact, it would seem that trance dancing and other ecstatic/vision-related endeavors may be easier by Her assistance.

Because the Graces are of such a high rank, being Goddesses themselves, They do not necessarily respond well to commands or demands by mortals who are seeking Their help. They have chosen to be in Aphrodite's service, but They are not servants. They prefer to be entreated for Their help, and They fully expect offering to be made to that end. These offerings should be physically (or lyrically) beautiful items, and it is best if they are cast into the sea. Also, Sappho notes in one of her poems, which is now known as fragment 13, "...for the blessed Graces too prefer things decked with flowers to gaze upon, and turn aside from those that are ungarlanded."

The Oreads are the other notable component of Aphrodite's retinue; however, there is very little written about the Oreads, either. So, once again, much of the information here is based on personal experience and meditation. They are very much like other nymphs, but there are some unique differences.

All nymphs share some basic qualities. They were known and honored as the spirits of specific natural features – certain mountains, rivers, and groves, were associated with particular types of nymphs. The nymphs are described as young women, and their name even derives from a word that means "young woman."

There seems to be some question about their mortality; however, there is one source in which a nymph specifically says how long her race lives. She likens their lives to the measure of generations of other creatures – the crow, man, stag, and phoenix. It works out to 3240 generations of men, which would certainly seem immortal to those of us who live long if we live ninety years. The Hamadryads, a type of nymph, each chose a tree. They are linked so closely with their chosen tree, it is said, that they die when the tree dies.

Nymphs have the power to change the shape of things – including people. They turned Hylas into an echo, and they have even been known to change human women into nymphs like themselves.

They can be aggressive lovers, as is shown in the abduction of Hylas and the killing of Hymnus. However, they can also be tender in their care of others. In fact, they have frequently been the nurses of the Gods, as with Zeus and Dionysos.

Sophocles, in his *Oedipus Tyrranus*, describes the Oreads as nymphs of Helicon with whom the Bacchants' God most often sports. By this, we are able to assume that Dionysos spends a great deal of time frolicking with them in the wooded hills where they dwell.

In *The Aeneid*, Virgil also mentions the Oreads. While Dido goes to the shrine, the Chorus says, "Diana leads Her bright processional; hither and yon are visionary legions of numberless Oreads." This indicates two things. First, the Oreads are also associated with Diana (Artemis). This isn't terribly surprising since they are nymphs of mountains, and some of Them are huntresses. Second, there are a great number of Them. Again, this isn't surprising since nymphs are abundant woodland creatures.

The Oreads are creative and imaginative. They are craftswomen, and Their craft is akin to that of the dwarves of other cultures. They are the keepers of jewels and gems found in Their hills. Specifically, They are the keepers of "found" gems and offer the Lady roughly cut and raw stones, especially raw rubies, sapphires, emeralds and diamonds. They crown Her with chaplets and garlands of wildflowers. With these wildflowers and rough gems, we are able to see a wilder, freer side of Aphrodite. (The other side of Her, which is sophisticated and coy, is decked in cut stones and finely wrought gold at the hands of Her husband.)

The Oreads dwell in grottoes, garden-like mountain caves. Although They are mountain nymphs, They are connected to the sea where mountains plunge into the ocean and in little coves and crevices where rivers and streams fall into the sea. The name Oread means mountain nymph.

The Graces and Oreads are not Aphrodite's only followers, though. In fact, Aphrodite is said to have followers of many varieties. For example, the figure of Desire is said to have followed Her at Her birth and ever after. Furthermore, a good number of Her followers were mortals whom she had helped.

Helen, the most beautiful mortal woman to have lived, was certainly among Her worshippers. In fact, Homer tells of an incident after She had rescued Alexandros (Paris) from certain death on the battlefield when the Goddess went to Helen and threatened to encompass her with "hard hate" if she did not go and comfort him. Needless to say, Helen complied without delay.

The daughters of Pandareos are said to be Her followers due to the help She gave them. Pausanias tells a story where Penelope says, "... the parents of the maidens died because of the wrath of the Gods, that they were reared as orphans by Aphrodite..." Sadly, when Aphrodite went to secure happy marriages for the girls, the Harpies carried them off and gave them to the Furies.

Jason and Medeia are both accounted among Aphrodite's human followers. Pausanias describes an artifact by saying, "Medeia is seated on a throne, while Jason stands on her right and Aphrodite on her left. On them is an inscription – 'Jason weds Medeia, as Aphrodite bids.'" Of this couple, Pindar also writes:

> "Aphrodite of Cyprus brought the maddening bird to men for the first time, and she taught the son of Aeson skill in prayerful incantation, so that he could rob Medea of her reverence for her parents ..."

Medea then told Jason how to meet the labors set by her father and gave him a potion.

There are other stories that are not so involved that also tell briefly of the mortals who worshipped her. Pausanias tells of Aphrodite's rescue of Creusa, one of the captive women in the sack of Troy. Lady Aphrodite rescued her from slavery among the Greeks because she was the wife of Her son, Aeneas. Sophocles, in *Oedipus Tyrannus*, tells how Aphrodite took Phaethon, who was like a God, and made him "keeper of Her shrine by night, a divine spirit." Furthermore, She gave Leilanion the golden apples that enabled him to distract and overtake Atalanta in a footrace, thereby winning her as wife. Aphrodite was involved in the creation of the infamous Pandora. In *Works and Days*, Hesiod says that each of the Olympians had a part in Pandora's making. Aphrodite "shed grace upon her head and cruel longing and cares that weary the limbs."

She also gave assistance to men in battle, although She had no power for fighting herself. Apollodorus tells of two incidents where She saved men from death in battle. She carried away Alexander (Paris) when he was bested in single combat by Menelaus and brought him to be comforted by Helen. She also rescued Butes (one of the Argonauts) by carrying him out of the water as he tried to swim to the Sirens.

NAMES

As Aphrodite Urania (meaning "Heavenly"), She is the representation of pure and spiritual love. As Pandemos ("Common" or "Of the People"), She represents physical satisfaction. However, these certainly can and should be viewed with subtler distinctions.

There are other names that give indications as to Aphrodite's nature, as well. Some of these names merely speak to Her birth or the places with which She is associated. "Rich crowned Cytherea" and "Cyprogenes" both deal with the two places that claim Her birth. "Foam-born Goddess" and "Philommedes" ("from genitals"), both relate to the most popular interpretation of the manner of Her birth. "Acidalia" is a name which means "from Her bath" and gives honor to Her in this aspect and reminds us of the importance of Her as a Goddess of cleansing and purification. (She frequently went to Her bath to wash away the unpleasantness of negative circumstances.)

Other names include:

Acraea	Of the Height
Aligena/Alugena	Sea-Born
Ambologera	Postponer of Old Age
Anadyomene	She Who Rises from the Waves
Androphonos	Man-Slayer
Antheia	Friend of Flowers
Apatouria	Deceitful
Aphrilis	"To Open" (the blooms of Spring)
Apostrophia	Rejecter (of sexual crimes)
Area	Armed for Battle
Asteria	Starry
Benetrix	Protector of Marriage
Callipygos	Beautiful Buttocks
Charis	Of the Graces/ Charities
Chrysheie	Radiant Like Gold
Columba	Dove
Cyprogenea	Born on Cypress

Despoena	Mistress/Lady
Doritis	Bountiful
Epistrophia	She Who Moves Men to Love
Epipontia	On the Sea
Epitymbria	She of the Tombs
Euploios	Fair Voyage
Gameli/Hymen	Marriage
Genetyllis/Ilithyia	Of Childbirth
Irene/Eirene	Dove of Peace
Kataskopia	Spying
Limenia	Of the Harbor
Margarete	Pearl
Maris/Pelagia/Stella	Of the Sea
Mechanitis	Deviser
Melaina/Skotia	Black or Dark One
Melissa	Queen Bee
Migonitis	Uniter
Morpho	Changing or Shapely
Paphia	Sexual Love
Pasiphae	Shining on All
Peitho	Persuasion
Philomedes	Laughter Loving
Porne	Patroness of Prostitutes
Praxis	Action
Psithyristes	Whispering

Using the information in this chapter, with the ritual outline as a base, I have created two Aphrodite rituals to share with others. They are a starting place for developing one's own "Liturgy of Grace."

Exercises

1. What elements of ritual appeal to you? Where do you feel like you need a stronger background?
2. Find a partner or a small group with whom you can practice the Sacred Touch Ceremony. Pay attention to your reactions to the experiences of both giving and receiving touch and pleasure in this way.
3. Keep notes regarding aspects of Aphrodite's myths and character to which you feel affiliated, curious or afraid. These are probably things you'll want to research and explore as your grow.

For Further Consideration

Burkert, Walter. Greek Religion. Harvard University Press, 1985.

> Great basic information about Greek religious beliefs and practices. Considered one of the foundational texts on the subject.

Alexander, Timothy Jay. A Beginner's Guide to Hellenismos. Lulu, 2007.

Alexander, Timothy Jay. Hellenismos Today. Lulu, 2007.

Fabulous introductory texts for Neo-Hellenic practice. These are great foundational resources for anyone wanting to approach Greek religion in a modern context.

CHAPTER 5
THE MIRROR RITUAL

NOW ROSE THE MOON, FULL AND ARGENTINE,
WHILE ROUND STOOD THE MAIDENS, AS AT A SHRINE.

- SAPPHO

NOTE: I've "Wiccanized" these ritual in this chapter and the one in the next chapter so that they may be approachable to the largest number of people.
Please feel at liberty to change any aspects of the rituals that you feel will make them more meaningful to you. The words of the calls and releases are only suggestions. The important thing is to say the words, make the gestures, play the music or do the dance that will speak to your inner mind.

TOOLS/SUPPLIES

- Illumination lanterns for the Quarters
- Shell
- Yellow apple
- Hammer
- Mirror
- Salt dough
- Toothpicks
- Sparkling apple cider
- Chocolates
- Cup & plate

- Staff

PURPOSE:

Honoring the beauty in ourselves in order to honor the beauty of Aphrodite

Call to Ritual – One participant (other than the Priest and Priestess) gathers the ritual celebrants together and says: "Aphrodite and Hephaestus await us that they may teach us a lesson of love. If you would proceed to the Rite, follow me."

All participants enter the ritual space and form a circle.

Lustration – The person who will later call Water/West walks around the group with a pitcher of water and an empty bowl. She pours water over the hands of each participant, catching the excess in the bowl. (This may be done with two people – one holds the bowl while the other pours the water.)

Establishing Sacred Space
Casting the Circle – The Priest and Priestess of the Rite walk in opposite directions around the space. One (or both) of them says: "We draw the circle

around us, an evocation of the temples and groves of our ancestors. Nothing is allowed within except that which we call."

East/Air: "We call to the Guardians of the East, creatures of Air and Intellect. Be with us and help us to understand the events that are about to enfold us."

South/Fire: "We call to the Guardians of the South, creatures of Fire and Passion. Be with us and help us to create a new reality based on what we experience."

West/Water: "We call to the Guardians of the West, creatures of Water and Emotion. Be with us and help us to feel the blessings inherent in this rite."

North/Earth: "We call to the Guardians of the North, creatures of Earth and Action. Be here with us and help us to move and work in the ways of love."

Welcome: The Priest or Priestess of the rite steps forward and says: "We have come together in this sacred place and time to learn a lesson of love at the hands of Aphrodite. We are here to look into the mirror and see the truth of our beauty. Are we able to proceed?"

All answer.

CALLING APHRODITE AND HER RETINUE

Hestia is called by the same individual who called Fire in the South: "We call Hestia, keeper of the hearth-fire and of the temple-fire. You are honored in all sacred spaces. Hestia, beloved Goddess of the sacred flame of life and light, enter this circle and make all within it holy." Light a candle on the main altar and say, "Hail, Hestia."

Oreads, place gifts of raw stones on the altar and say: "To Aphrodite's retinue we call. Oreads, you nymphs of mountains and grottoes – dance through this company and bring your glittering magic to this circle. Be with us as we discover our own beauty."

Graces, place gifts of jewelry on the altar and say: "Graces: Splendor, Mirth and Good Cheer – we come to learn the lessons of your lady, Aphrodite Kypris! Bless this circle and these worshippers with your gifts of beauty, laughter, and happiness. Aglaea, Euphrosyne, and

Thalia, be near!"

Hephaestus, the Priest of the Rite: "Hephaestus, forge God and most fortunate husband of Aphrodite, hear us. You are the maker of wonders. Come to us from your volcanic workshop, the Earth's primal forge, and teach us the truths of your love for your lady. We will learn them, Hephaestus, and we will walk in the knowledge and wisdom forever."

Aphrodite, the Priestess of the Rite: "Beautiful Lady Aphrodite! Shod in foam, crowned in seashells and sunshine Resplendent One. Lady of Love. Cytherea, Kypris, Aphrodite Urania. Of the cypress and the apple grove. We honor you, and we ask you to come to us. Teach us the limitless bounty of your love. We walk in your light, and we will live in your love."

THE DRAMA

Hephaestus stands near the South/Fire and holds the staff.

Hephaestus: "I am a smith, the God of the Forge. A volcano is my forge fire, full of power and heat. Yet my Lady's love seems

cool. I bend metal and shape it to my will. Yet I am called lame and crippled. Who would know me and love what she sees?"

Aphrodite (standing in the West/Water): "Husband, I am here. What do you ask of me?"

Hephaestus: "Love, I have heard rumors that you do not love me. Most Beautiful, it is said that my sooty hands and lame legs repulse you. Delightful One, is it truly spoken that you find me dull? Why are you with me?"

Aphrodite: "My love is misunderstood again, I see. Hephaestus, I know the love you bear to me. I've seen its proof in your eyes. Your love has no limits or rules. You shower me with jewels because you see the beauty in my face. You adorn me with fine metalwork because you find pleasure with my body. You have delighted me with the love you gave so freely."

Hephaestus: "It is no secret that I love you. How can I resist Love herself? No one can. But, Wife, I ask you: How do you love me?"

Aphrodite: "You have given me gifts – both beautiful and powerful. It is my turn to give a gift to you." (Holds mirror before him)

Hephaestus: "A mirror? Who wants to look upon the face of the one whose own mother cast him out because she found him ugly?"

Aphrodite: "You, of all the Gods of Olympus, have the trained eye to see the details. Use your skill to distinguish the beauty of my dear husband."

"Beauty does not sit on the surface of a face or a body. True beauty shines through it. Your beauty is in your imagination, your heart and your hands. Sooty and calloused as they seem, lustrous beauty shines in all they create.

"I delight in your gifts and your talents. I love your capacity to love me so deeply. But until you love yourself, you deny the greatest portion of your love.

"Accept my gift, dear one, and look deeply. Find your own beauty and love what you see. In so doing, you give honor and love back to me."

Hephaestus (looks into mirror, then says): "Truly, the hardest person to love is the one who peers at you through the glass each morning. And yet, only upon recognizing beauty there, can you really see it elsewhere."

THE WORK

Priest: "As the priestess of the rite brings the mirror to you, see the beauty that is yours. See your talents, your joys, your gifts, your loves, your passions, your pride, your purpose. See the beauty that shines in your face and your body, your mind and your spirit. Acknowledge, accept and love ALL the beauty you see. It is a part of your Divinity. Delight in it. Honor it."

"Begin to honor it daily. Now is the best time to start. After you have seen yourself, express your beauty in a portion of this salt dough. Sculpt the dough, if you like. Use these toothpicks as writing utensils to inscribe words or symbols that express the beauty you already possess."

The Priestess holds the mirror to each person in the circle, as the Priest holds up the lantern (from the South Quarter) for each to see.

Priestess: "Your own beauty, and the ability to see it, is a great gift from Aphrodite herself. Offer it back to her now, and you will begin to understand the true nature of Love and Beauty and the Lady Aphrodite."

Cast sculptures into the water (or fire) as tokens of offering.

LIBATION

Libation of sparkling cider and chocolates. The Priest and/or priestess says: "We rejoice in the sweetness of Aphrodite's love. We revel in the beauty She has shown us. Thank you, Lady and Lord, for revealing what lies below the layers of our images and helping us to see the beauty and love that we carry."

Pour cider in a controlled manner to the ground (or bowl). Drop chocolates in the same place. Then share the remainder of the libation with the celebrants.

RELEASE THE SACRED

Each participant can speak a variation on the following in order to thank and release the entities that they called: "We thank you for your presence and your blessings. We are grateful for the protections that you've extended to us. Withdraw now, and come back again with our honor when the time is appropriate."

EXERCISES
(See Chapter 6)

CHAPTER 6
THE APHRODISIA RITUAL

COME HITHER FOAM-BORN CYPRIAN GODDESS, COME,

AND IN GOLDEN GOBLETS POUR RICHEST NECTAR

ALL MIXED IN MOST ETHEREAL PERFECTION,

THUS TO DELIGHT US.

—SAPPHO

SET UP

<u>Main altar</u> – Incense burner, charcoal, Aphrodite incense, elemental symbols (candles, blade, wand, plate of salt, bowl of water), oil lamp/candle (for Hestia), cream puffs ("cakes")

<u>Aphrodite altar</u> – icon/image of the Goddess, seashells, blue altar cloth, large clamshell with water (for lustration), apple branch (spurge), dove images, golden apple (the real, edible fruit), golden inscribed apple, chalice of apple cider ("ale"), pitcher of water, temple images, space for offerings, golden apple talismans, packets of Aphrodite Bath Salts for all, picture and candle for Graces, picture and candle for Oreads

<u>Anaktoron</u> (innermost sanctum of the temple) – marked on the floor/ground with light blue, dark blue, and white cords and rose petals, votive candle at each corner – red (passion), blue (sea/bath), yel-

low (gold), white (seafoam)

<u>Participants</u> – drums, rattles, music-makers; offerings to Aphrodite

SCRIPT/OUTLINE

Vow of Silence – Administered by the Heralds (Adonis and Sappho)

Spoken by Adonis – "You are preparing to enter the Rites of the Aphrodisia. This is a mystery ritual, and as a participant in it, you will be initiated into these Mysteries of Aphrodite. Everything that you experience and witness here is sacred. Mystery is not understood by those who have not experienced it, and the price paid for breaking the vow of silence is a high one. The price will not be extracted by us, but by Aphrodite herself."

Spoken by Sappho – "Never break a women's confidence. Her wrath can destroy as completely as her love can heal."

Together – "Will you honor the silence of the Mystery?" *(All who answer "yes" will continue. All who answer "no" or give no answer will leave, in love and honesty and integrity.)*

"Then prepare to enter the Aphrodisia."

Lustration – Hydranos Priestess (Water/West caller), *using the water in the clamshell, she cleanses and blesses each participant by anointing the third eye:*
"Eye of spirit where wisdom enters ..."
Anoints palm of right hand:
"May Her love enter from the right hand ..."
Anoints palm of left hand:
"May Her beauty enter from the left hand ..."
Anoints heart:
"For She dwells within ..."
Sprinkles whole body:
"And without ..."
Touches chin:
"In beauty ..."
Bows head:
"And honor..."
Raises arms:
"Hail!"

(Note: The above lustration is an adaptation of the lusral rite included in Jennifer Reif's *Demeter*.)

As each participant enters the circle and takes his/her place, they can pick up drums and other instruments and begin drumming softly until all are in circle. The lustration should begin with "Sappho" and "Adonis" and end with the Hiereia (Aphrodite).

Raising the Grove – Hiereia Aphroditus (Aphrodite's Priestess), *using the water in the clamshell*
"To the sacred grove I call –
Ancient trees one and all.
Apple, olive, myrtle, cypress
Form this sacred place for us.
Over our heads and below our feet,
Your branches, trunks, and roots will meet.
By the power of three times three
As I will it, so mote it be."

Calling the Quarters

Call using any words that are comfortable to you. Include the tools and symbols of the Quarter. (You may use the words from the Mirror Ritual, if you like).

Please note that if you don't have enough different people to carry out the roles for the entire ritual, the Quarter-Callers may "double" in the following ways:

East/Air – *The caller of East is also the Hieraules (leads the music).*

.

North/Earth – *The caller of North is also the Priest/Priestess of Hecate.*

West/Water – *The caller of West is also the Hydranos Priest/Priestess.*

South/Fire – *The caller of South is also the Porphyros (keeper of the sacred flame) and the Priest/Priestess of Hestia.*

Welcome – Priest/Priestess of Hecate (North/ Earth caller)

Holding aloft the seashell used in cleansing the circle and in the lustration:

"We stand here together at the beginning of the Aphrodisia and the Mystery Rites of Aphrodite. Have we all come to honor Her?"

All answer.

"Have we all come with love and reverence?"

All answer.

"Will you always hold these Mysteries sacred?"

All answer.

"Have the offerings been brought?"

All answer.

"Then let us begin the Aphrodisia."

Evocation of Hestia – Pyrphoros (South/Fire caller)

Steps to main altar and says:

"We call Hestia,
Goddess of the hearth and temple fire,
Of the spiritual center of our world,
and of all sacred places.
Hestia, beloved Goddess of the spiritual flame,
Come and enter this temple.
Make all that is here holy and sacred in Your name.
Bring us the peace and sureness of that place which is home and hearth.
Bring your purity and beauty to us
As we honor You,
who are the center of the spiritual flame.
So mote it be."

Lights the candle (or oil lamp) for Hestia, raises it up and says:

"Hail, Hestia!"

Evocation of Aphrodite's Retinue

Oreads – placing gifts of raw stones on the altar and lighting the candle, say:
"To Aphrodite Acidalia's retinue I call! Oreads: you nymphs of mountains and grottoes – Dance through this company and bring your glittering magic to this grove. Be with us as we discover Her love and beauty! So mote it be!"

Graces – placing gifts of jewelry on the altar and lighting the candle, say:
"Graces: Splendor, Mirth and Good Cheer – We come to honor your lady, Aphrodite Kypris! Bless this grove and these worshippers with your gifts of beauty, laughter, and happiness. Aglaea, Euphrosyne, and Thalia, be near!
So mote it be!"

Invocation of Sappho – by Adonis
Use the words that come to you in the moment. Remember Sappho's qualities: physical beauty, compassion, tenderness, eroticism, appreciation of women AND men, gorgeous poetry. Call her as a lover of Aphrodite.

Invocation of Adonis – by Sappho
Use the words that come to you in the moment. Remember Adonis' qualities: vibrant youth,

erotic sexuality, devotion, compassion. Call him as a lover of Aphrodite.

Invocation of Aphrodite – by Sappho and Adonis

Spoken by Sappho – "Beautiful Lady Aphrodite! Shod in foam, crowned in seashells and sunshine. Resplendent One, Lady of Love, Cytherea, Kypris, Aphrodite Urania. Lady of the cypress and the apple grove."

Spoken by Adonis – "Enter grace, enter beauty, enter the heart into ecstasy!"

Spoken by Sappho – "Aphrodite! Take this, the body of your priestess. Become incarnate through her. Let her voice echo your words. Let her hands do your work. Let her countenance mirror your beauty."

Spoken by Adonis – "Enter grace, enter beauty, enter the heart into ecstasy!"

Spoken by Sappho – "Aphrodite, be here now!"

Spoken by Adonis – "Enter grace, enter beauty, enter the heart into ecstasy!"

The Hieraules (musician/East caller) leads the group in a chant of "Ela ... Dea Orea" ("Come,

... beautiful Goddess") until possession is achieved.

Dromena – Prologue – spoken by Adonis

"Perhaps you have never heard the story of Aphrodite and the Golden Apple. "

"It happened when all the Gods of Olympos were gathered to celebrate the wedding of Peleus and Thetis. One had been neglected. This one was Strife, and She would have Her presence felt."

"So She took a golden apple and inscribed it with the words 'For the Fairest.' Three Goddesses, all having a valid claim, vied for the trophy. To avoid heartache, Zeus appointed Paris of Troy to decide who would win it."

"Each Goddess offered a bribe. Hera, Queen of the Gods, offered lands and power. Athena, the Wise Warrior, offered victory in battle. Aphrodite, mother of Persuasion, offered Helen as bride. He chose Helen, wife of Menelaus and most beautiful of all mortal women, and the Trojan War began."

"So, the Golden Apple rolled in, and competition, confusion, and contention began."

Dromena

Sappho sits, writing a poem – "My Love, I await you in this cypress grove. Wrap me in your embrace ..."

Adonis enters, notices the apple lying nearby on the ground, and picks it up. He says – "My love comes here soon, Sappho. I know she'll want us to be alone."

Sappho – "I have no intention of interfering with your plans, but my lover has always met me in this grove. We will need our privacy and this grove is special to us, Adonis. I am sure your lady won't mind going further off."

Adonis, still trying to maintain composure despite growing irritation – "The grove is sacred to us, as well, and my Lady made much of our meeting <u>here</u>. Do you wish to defy the Lady Cytherea?"

Sappho, getting testier, too – "Clearly not, as I strive against distraction to keep my appointed place. She bade me stay <u>here</u> for her, and stay I shall!"

Adonis, thinking he has found an explanation – "Ah. I see. She has asked you to stand guard that none may disturb our private revels. Very well, you may stay, so long as you stay outside the grove." He makes a gesture of dismissal.

Sappho is very put off by his words and his gesture – "How dare you, boy! Aphrodite has asked me to be here for herself. Perhaps you are the guard at the gate that none may disturb us. Be gone! She comes."

Aphrodite enters, and addresses them both with gestures of love and affection – "Hello, dear ones. I am pleased to see you both. Thank you for keeping vigil and meeting me here."

Adonis – "Lady, I understand that you have many lovers, and I am not a jealous man. But I looked forward to our meeting here this night. I am certain you prefer a man's love, and this woman is in the way of our pleasure."

Sappho – "Silly, boy. You know not the ecstasy one woman can give another. It is evident our sweet lady wants me to stay, and not you. Now, go before you regret your words and actions here tonight."

Aphrodite – "My dear loves, it is nonsense for either of you to pretend to know my heart. I will always determine who I want and when I want them for myself. Do not presume that I have erred in asking you both here, for indeed I haven't."

Adonis, beginning to enjoy the idea of bedding both Aphrodite and Sappho – "So you have called us here that we may all have pleasure together?"

Aphrodite – "Yes, but don't jump to conclusions, Adonis. My, you are an eager youth! I want the pleasure of your company, the pleasure of your laughter, the pleasure of dancing and feasting with you. There is more pleasure than just sexuality – although I may decide I want that pleasure, too. But it will be my choice, and only one of many pleasures to be found. Strike drum! and dance with me. Lose yourself in the ecstasy and the pleasure of dance and drink and all that is sweet." *She feeds each of them a strawberry and gives each a taste of cider.*

Aphrodite coaxes both lovers into dancing while music plays (drumming); She brings the whole assembly into ecstatic drumming and dancing. During this time, honey, chocolate, apple cider, wine are all enjoyed, and Sappho and Adonis (if not everyone else) gets messy. The messiness begins as merely playful and then more competitive. (The Priest and Priestesses are directing the group's energy through all this to the bowl of apple talismans on the altar.)

After a time, Aphrodite begins to bathe herself by washing her face and hands. Then, She does the same for Sappho and Adonis.

Then, She leads the group through a pathworking of Her bath. (The bath is symbolic of smoothing and taming the chaos and strife by reaffirming love and acts of beauty.)

> *Aphrodite* – "In symbol, I have bathed myself and Adonis and Sappho. The bath itself is a symbol and a Mystery. Although your body cannot go to my sacred bathing place in Cypress, your mind and spirit can. Close your eyes now as I take you there."

> "As you relax, you notice a thick mist approaching along the ground. You cannot see through it. It is cool and inviting. It creeps to your feet, enveloping them. As the mist touches your feet, they are more relaxed. You take no more notice of them. The mist climbs up your legs, and they

relax too. The smooth, cool mist climbs up your buttocks and your torso and you know they are relaxed. Your chest, your neck, your face and head, all wrapped in mist."

"As you look around, and see only mists, you know you are between times and between lands. You can barely see your feet when you look down at them, but they are there. You test the ground with your foot to see if it is steady. It is."

"Very vaguely, just a few feet away, you see the shape of a young woman. She approaches and takes your hand. As she leads you down the very smooth path, you think you notice little horns on her head. The mist is thick, though, and you can't be sure."

"She leads you steadily down the sloping path. You trust her. Although you sense her playfulness, you know she will not lead you astray."

"The path becomes sandy and the mists begin to separate a bit. You can see that you are on a beach. Suddenly, you emerge into bright sunlight. The sun is golden in the sky, and it shines brilliantly upon the clear, blue water. To your right, not far down the beach, you see a temple built high up on the rocks. There is a staircase that spirals down from the smooth temple floor to the smooth sandy beach. There are several women walking down the stairs. You notice, too, that there are several on the beach."

"The young Oread who has been guiding you, tugs at your hand once more. This time when you look at her, you are sure that you see little horns on her head. You walk by her side, still holding her hand, until you are in the midst of the women at the sea."

"'You have arrived safely,' one of them says to you. The women are all of different groups. There are some like your guide, woodsy and wild and beautiful. Some of these have horns and some do not. Some are robed in white chittons with blue-green trim or yellow trim or pink trim. Three of the women are clad in graceful drapes of sheer white, trimmed in gold, with golden bracelets and necklaces. Their hair is beautifully piled on their heads with a few ringlets framing their faces."

"Of these three, one is tall and slender, one is of average height and voluptuous, and the other is quite young. The youngest smiles at you with a radiance that you have never seen, and you feel the need to giggle. The other two begin to remove your clothes, and you feel a twinge of embarrassment at the condition of your robes. They are humble in comparison to their fine raiment, but this is not where you feel any sting of shame. Rather, you feel the dirtiness of the stains on your clothing. They haven't been properly washed in such a long time, although this seems to be the first time you have noticed."

"The stains on your clothes are there because of choices that you have made, and this is what embarrasses you. You look at the clothing of the women around you. No matter what their status or nature, how humble their clothing, it is all clean."

"You are glad to be free of your clothing, and you notice the Oread who lead you here is now carefully washing them in the clear, clean water."

"Then you notice how dirty you are. In this clear, golden light by the sea, you are able to see the marks that your toils and fortunes have left upon your feet, your hands, your heart, your face. You feel a great deal of sadness. In some places, you have scars, but the scars don't sadden you. The soot that covers the scars is troubling your heart. A few tears streak the dirt on your face."

"The tall, slender woman, Euphrosyne (Mirth), wipes the tears from your cheeks. She says, 'Yes, salt water can clean this away.' She leads you into the water. The voluptuous Aglaea is on the other side of you. Thalia, the youngest, is behind you. The waters are calm and soothing. You allow the Graces to bathe you."

"After they have finished, they lead you back to the shore. When you are on the soft, warm sand, the young nymph brings your clothes to you. The three Sisters put them on you and comb your hair. When they have finished, you notice your skin and raiment again. It is shining and clean. You are glowing with your own light, and nothing hinders it from shining now."

"The Oread that lead you here approaches you again, but before you go one of the Graces has a message. She also has a gift, a small golden apple that she places in your palm."

"You thank her for her generosity by giving her a kiss. Then you turn to the Oread again. She walks with you back to the edge of the mist, and you see the path that leads you here. She stops and doesn't walk with you, but you know the path. You walk along the straight, gentle climb, surrounded again by the thick mist. As the mist clears, you see the candle light of this grove. You see your body waiting for you, and before you realize that you have made the choice to return, you are back."

"Take moment to find your limbs again, and stand when you are ready."

Dromena – Epilogue – spoken by Sappho

"Strife came to the marriage feast with an apple as a gift of chaos. She hoped to unsettle love and wreck the happiness of a joyful union. She brought contention and competition and confusion."

"But Lady Aphrodite uses love and beauty to heal these hurts and smooth these problems. Loving words can untangle confusion. A loving touch can ease contention. A loving smile can erase competition."

"So Aphrodite claims the symbol of the apple, and makes it Hers. Truly, Love Conquers All Things."

SEALING THE WORK

Each participant will come individually to the Anaktoron to be bathed by Aphrodite, Adonis and Sappho. As they do this, the other members are drumming and chanting "Acidalia, Dea Orea."

As each participant leaves the Anaktoron, s/he walks the circle of the sacred space one full time and goes to Aphrodite's altar. At the altar, s/he will place his/her offering there and say any words that are appropriate. After s/he has left the offering, s/he will take water from the shell to bathe the Aphrodite icon, then anoint the icon with the rose oil. When all this is done, the participant will take one of the golden apples that have been inscribed with the words "For the fairest" and "Amor Vincit Omnia."

Spoken by the Priestess of Aphrodite – "These apples have been empowered by the energy of the Rite. They will serve as talismans for you – reminders of the power of Love and Beauty and symbols of Aphrodite Acidalia, She who rises from Her bath in the sea. Keep them and remember your vow."

Libation

      Cakes – cream puffs
      Ale – Apple cyser

Release Aphrodite – Spoken by Sappho

      "Aphrodite Urania
Aphrodite Acidalia
We thank you for your presence here, sweet lady.

It is time now to depart the body of your priestess.

Leave her gently, Adored One.
Most beautiful among the Goddesses!
Return now to your temple by the sea.
Return to your attendants of old who await you.

Hail and farewell."

Release the Sacred (in reverse order from the way it was called.)

ƐXƐRCIƧƐƧ

1. If you can find other celebrants to enter the two rituals here with you, huzzah! Feel free to modify where needed to make the rituals your own. If you can't engage in the rituals with others, re-work them for solitary practice.

2. Record your perceptions from these (and other) rituals in your journal.

3. Start jotting down any ideas that you may have

for Aphrodisian Rites. You can keep them in their own notebook or flag them in your journal in some way.

CHAPTER 7
CULTIVATING GRACE

Grace and charm are ideas that are often associated with Aphrodite, and I have come to believe that an Aphrodisian woman, let alone a Priestess of Aphrodite, would be embodiments of these ideas. I think she should work to cultivate them in the same way that a gardener cultivates the most beautiful of roses in the garden.

The Graces of the Greek pantheon bear names that mean Splendor, Mirth and Good Cheer. In order to cultivate a persona of grace, then, a Priestess of Aphrodite might look to these names as a roadmap of the qualities that she can develop.

I don't know that any one quality is more important than another, but I do find it notable that the Graces embody two traits of personality and only one of physicality. Interpret this how you will, but it seems to me that a woman who isn't traditionally "beautiful" has nothing to fear in terms of not living up to Aphrodite's standards. "Beauty" is only part of the equation.

SPLENDOR

I don't actually think that "splendor" and "beauty" are the same quality, to tell the truth. They may be related, even closely related, but there are some differences. Beauty is all about the physical features and how an individual or a society interprets them. Splendor, I think, is perhaps a quality or attribute of beauty, but works on a slightly different system. Beauty my fade with time, because it is a gift of nature. Splendor, though, can always be put on. It can be honed and refined, like a skill.

Splendor is that indefinable "something" about a person that makes her physically captivating. I've heard it described as an "aura" – sometimes sexual – that draws people in. Women that may not fit society's definitions of beauty may be splendid, all the same. Men are attracted to them, and women recognize them as alluring.

Maya Angelou wrote about this in her poem, "Phenomenal Woman." The speaker says that she isn't cute or built like a fashion model, but men are still drawn to her. She credits this appeal to her laugh, her walk, and the swing of her hips. Her confidence and her joy are what attract the people around her. The same is true for Aphrodite's Women.

The truth is that most men and women can accept,

with maturity, that the version of beauty that is foisted upon us from the fashion industry and the media doesn't do much to encompass the real beauty of men and women. If you haven't figured that out yet – if you're still trying to force yourself into the cookie cutter model of beauty – let it go. Give up someone else's ideals of glamour and splendor, and begin to wear he splendor of yourself.

Now, all this isn't to say that developing splendor is an entirely natural process. Some part of it that "aura" might come naturally, but the rest might take some attention on your part. I know it does on mine.

The trick is finding the aspects of splendor that appeal to you and work well for you. We each have our different strengths and natural proclivities in this area.

Dance is an area in which I cultivate splendor, for example. I started bellydancing several years ago, and I have found it to be a wonderful medium for expressing my joy, passion, lust, playfulness and more. I can't say that I pursue terribly authentic forms of Middle Eastern dance, which is why I always use the term "bellydance." For me, the dance is a fusion of movements that express what I am feeling.

It also helps me connect with the music, and it becomes a form of role-playing, in that. I can put on the character of a certain kind of woman – or a woman in certain circumstances – and play that out through the language of dance and music.

Dance is a connection for me to Aphrodite's service in a direct way. I dance in honor of Her, and I have danced for Her pleasure. When I dance, I know that I command the attention of the audience, and I am aware of the sometimes visceral and intense reactions they can have to the swaying and undulating of my body.

I dance for myself, alone and unwatched, as a way to connect with Aphrodite. I can feel Her sensuality and Her confidence in my hips and ribs and feet. My hands echo Her grace, and I know that it is a perfect way for me to emulate Her.

Another way that anyone can cultivate splendor is through the development of a personal style or "look." Find the clothes and colors that help you feel the most attractive and alluring. They don't have to be in vogue, and they don't have to be a size 6. For the love of Kypris, they do NOT have to be skin-tight to be sexy, either.

In fact, "sexy" isn't the only Aphrodisian look. Anything that makes you feel confident and empowered will be right. It doesn't matter if nobody else is drawn to the specific clothes. If you feel good, they will be drawn to you in the clothes.

For myself, I have always felt the most comfortable and attractive in what I might call an eclectic palate. At the beginning of my high school career (1989), I discovered that I felt freer and more energized when I wore odd pieces together – mismatched, vintage, and "boy" pieces were my favorites. Since I wasn't conforming to the norms in fashion, it was like I'd released myself from the standards the rest of the world was trying to live by. I was the best/coolest/prettiest of what I was, and there was no longer any need to compare myself with the fashion plates who all looked the same – "perfect" maybe, but the same.

My tastes have changed over the years, and I have forgotten the power of embracing "my looks," as I've struggled to fit into professional dress codes. When I try to fit into the molds of "career woman" or "soccer mom," though, I always feel inadequate. With time, I come back to my own little funky style, and I feel splendid again.

MIRTH

As one of the Graces of personal, or interpersonal, interactions, Mirth is a Goddess of humor and joy. Euphrosyne embodies the characteristics of engaging people in pleasant conversations, capturing their imaginations and putting them at ease.

Not everyone is immediately talented at this art of

conversation. Some people are too uncomfortable in social situations to know how their partners are feeling, let alone to engage them adequately and put them at ease.

Charm can be developed, though. All it really takes is paying attention to people. Ask questions, listen to the answers, and, every now an then, think of and contribute an appropriate reply. Really, this last bit about coming up with something appropriate to say isn't a full third of this three part process. Most people will feel great about a conversation if you let them talk while they know that you're listening.

Another tip for engaging with people and putting them at ease is called "mirroring." Basically, the idea is that you match the other person's tone of voice, volume, excitement level, posturing/ positioning, facial expressions, etc. Most people will have no idea that you're doing it; they'll just notice how comfortable they are talking to you. They'll be comfortable because you will remind them of themselves, and the old adage really is true: "Birds of a feather flock together." The other birds will be happier if you show them how similar your feathers are.

GOOD CHEER

The youngest, and therefore most playful, of the Graces is Thalia. Good cheer, fun and happiness, are the easiest of the qualities of grace to cultivate. How hard is it to be happy?

Okay, if you're sitting there being glum and dour and thinking that your happiness is not within your own control, cheerfulness may seem like the quality that is the farthest from your ability to grasp. However, I have a shocking thought for you to ponder. Ready for it? Here it is:

You decide how you feel.

Nobody else around you has control over that. They may set up circumstances that influence the way you're going to react, but they don't make you either happy or unhappy. Only you can control that.

It's a mind-bender, that realization, and you may not be ready for it. When you are, though – when you can accept that you are in control of your joy – you'll find that you have a lot more of it. After all, when it's a choice of being content or being despondent, of being empowered or being powerless, of being cheerful or being mournful, who wouldn't choose "content, empowering, cheerfulness?"

Of course, you might still appreciate some solid techniques for bringing good cheer to yourself. Naturally, once you have it for yourself, you share it with others. Though you can't control how someone else feels, and therefore you can't "make" someone else happy, you've probably already noticed that good moods are contagious. If you're cheerful, the people around you are likely to be cheerful, as well.

Therein lies tip #1: Surround yourself with people who are happy, content, cheery, empowered. Remember the "birds of a feather?" Well, let's just say that plumage rubs off. It'll be harder for you to be down in the dumps if you stick close to folks who are uplifted and positive.

Another suggestion is to do the things you enjoy as much of the time as you can. Do work that fulfills you. Fill your free time with activities that bring you joy. If you can't do both, pick and choose those places where you can enjoy yourself.

My final tip is to laugh whenever you can. Watch comedians on tv, watch funny movies, play with little kids and listen to what they say. That'll make you smile, for sure. If it comes down to it, just sit and smile or laugh on purpose, without a stimulus. Just hold a smile and try to stay mad or morose. I dare you.

ƐXƐRCISƐS

1. Splendor – Spend some time identifying your strengths associated with the Grace Aglaea. What about you do others see as splendid? What about yourself do you see this way? What activities or actions appeal to you that

seem to fall under this Grace's domain?

2. Mirth – Reflect on the qualities of mirth in your life and character. Are you strong in this already? What could you do to increase this area?

3. Good Cheer – Enter into the same type of reflection for Thalia. How do you already honor this Grace? How can you embrace her qualities even further?

FOR FURTHER CONSIDERATION

Cameron, Julia. <u>The Artist's Way</u>. Tarcher, 2002.

> This book takes the approach that we are all inherently creative beings. The exercises and essays are designed to open you up to the creative forces in the Universe moving through you. There is an inherent connection between this work and the touch of the Charites.

CHAPTER 8
THE ART OF PLEASURE

NOW LOVE, THE INELUCTABLE, WITH BITTER SWEETNESS
FILLS ME, OVERWHELMS ME, AND SHAKES MY BEING.
NOW LIKE A MOUNTAIN WIND THE OAKS O'ERWHELMING,
EROS SHAKES MY SOUL.

- SAPPHO

I genuinely believe that the exploration of the art of pleasure could be a book unto itself. In reality, it is. In fact, there are hundreds of books dedicated to the idea of developing a zestful appreciation of the many acts of pleasure.

Pleasure encompasses so many realms of human experience, though, that we might spend a little time reflecting on the fact that all of the pleasures in the world are sensuous ways to revel in Aphrodite's bountiful gifts. After all, sex and erotica are not the only pleasures that do Her honor, and we would be neglectful not to intoxicate ourselves with the wine of pleasurable thought, at least for a moment.

FOOD AND DRINK

Oh, tasty tidbits are such a delight! Learning to truly enjoy food and drink of all varieties must be one of the many ways to receive joy. I'm not a gourmet cook myself – nor any type of cook, if I'm being honest – but I can enjoy an array of epicurean delights as well as the next girl.

The truth is: I love food. I haven't met a cuisine that I didn't enjoy. The way each culture spices and seasons, heats and chills, and presents their meals is a pleasurable feast for all the senses.

The French pride themselves on being connoisseurs of fine food and wine, and I know that one of the primary traits for judging any type of food is to savor it as fully as possible. Take in the colors and visual textures of a dish, the way you might appraise a work of art. Linger over the aromas. Contemplate the textures and tastes of each bite as you eat.

Really, eating is a process that we all share. Everyone must consume food and water to stay alive. If you don't have access to any other stimuli for pleasurable practice, you do have access to food. Start finding the pleasure in the meal, no matter how simple or ordinary it may be.

Prepare (or otherwise find) culinary experiences that speak to your own personal pleasure palate. Spend some time discovering your joys within the realm of food, and then spend some time delighting in those tastes, textures, sights and smells. Don't take food and drink for granted, as if they were truly only the equivalent of the fuel that you put in your car to keep it running. They can sustain your heart and soul as much as your body, if you let them.

Finally, of course, we have the interesting and exciting topic of Aphrodisiacs. Abundant source material exists to document love-inducing foods and drinks in every culture dating back to antiquity. These foods are usually shaped like either male or female genitalia, or they are inherently sensual and rich in flavor and texture. In same cases, chemical compounds are present that encourage or heighten a sexual response when ingested. Before using any Aphrodisiacs that aren't part of your normal diet, do your research and consult with a medical professional to make sure that it is safe for you based on any medical conditions you may have.

HOME COMFORTS

Housekeeping and decorating may not strike you immediately as Aphrodisian endeavors, but they certainly can be. For one thing, I can't imagine that Aphrodite would feel terribly welcome in a bare, spare and dingy abode. For another, I know from experience that it is hard to feel lovely and loveable when your surroundings are uninspiring or unkempt.

Don't get me wrong. I'm not preaching domesticity as a proper and traditional function that anyone, women in particular, should adhere to. There are certain pleasures to keeping a home clean and inviting, but those pleasures taken entirely for their own merits might fall into the sphere of another Goddess's influence – maybe Hestia's, for example.

However, there is a charm and grace to creating a pleasurable environment for yourself, your family, and your guests. Consider this aspect of housekeeping to be an extension of the role of Mirth in your life. Sit in a tidy, aesthetically pleasing room, and you will feel worlds happier than if that same room were in utter disarray.

Actually, the appointments of the room (the decorating and design) are very much within the sphere of Aphrodite's realm. When we pick colors for our walls, floors and furniture, we are setting a mood. We enhance this mood with textures that are evocative on both a visual and a tactile level. We sprinkle pictures and knick-knacks throughout the scene to further reinforce the theme, and these items also bring a part of our personalities and proclivities into the physical space. Maybe we light candles or incense to add a hint of olfactory delight. We choose lighting that casts the entire space with a brightness or glow that forces us to look through a specific lens. All of this is sensual, and therefore within the art of pleasure.

One of the appeals in decorating my own home has been the ability to establish different moods in the various rooms. One room can lean toward opulence, where another is very homey. One bathroom might be fresh, bright and spa-like, with another reminding me of a starlet's dressing room in the golden age of Hollywood. A guest bedroom might be comfortable and inviting, but my own bedroom gives the feel of walking into the giparu (the sacred bedchamber of the "En Priestess" in ancient Sumeria). All of the settings are pleasurable, but they allow for a variety of pleasures.

VISUAL ARTS

Anyone who has studied visual art, even as a child in public school, knows that there is so much going on in a visual piece. Color, line, movement, and texture are all present, and they combine to create a holistic, sensual experience.

Learning how to analyze and understand the world of art might very well increase one's repertoire of pleasure, since people tend to respond so readily to visual stimuli.

Applying the principles of visual art in daily life isn't a tricky task to accomplish. We each do it everyday, however unwittingly. We choose clothing, apply make-up, arrange our workspaces, and decorate our homes with whatever understanding of color, line, movement and texture that we already possess. These tasks might be more effective if we took the time to understand, appreciate and become fluent in the visual pleasures.

Aphrodite has a keen association with the Arts, and She always has. The Muses have had connections to Her in various myths and stories before there were considered to be nine of them. (The earliest tales of the Muses count their number as three – and sometimes as few as one.) It comes as no surprise that She is linked with these Goddesses of Inspiration when She has always been the subject of so much artistic effort. Her face and body have adorned sculpture, pottery and paintings since the earliest images of Deity have appeared. She has been honored in poem and song. Her touch commands such inspiration that even the women who most resemble Her loving, beautiful, and sexual natures are immortalized in the arts by the sculptors, painters, composers, poets and storytellers of their times.

Music

Our lives are enriched by music. For some, the drumbeat is akin to the heartbeat, and they would be lost without a world of rhythm and melody. For others, music is a finishing touch in an overall world of the senses. For all of us, music is evocative of the wide range of human emotion and experience. I don't believe that a theme, feeling, or circumstance has escaped the grasp of the musician.

Music provides us with a method of developing a

sense of pleasure in the auditory world, as well. We can create musical arrangements (on our mp3 players, if we aren't musicians ourselves) that speak to a certain mood. We can, and should, even listen outside of our usual genres to develop an appreciation for the sounds and arrangements that are pleasurable to others.

Furthermore, music heightens the experience of so many settings, it's no wonder that love scenes in movies are set to thrilling soundtracks that quicken the pulse and enliven the libido. Most adept ritualists have a keen understanding of the importance of music and its connection to higher awareness. Music has been used to set the mood in ceremonies and rites far pre-dating Aphrodisian temples, but you can bet that the Rites of Aphrodite were heralded with flutes, finger cymbals, lyres or other instruments and songs.

DANCE

Dance is the body's poetry. I hope that doesn't sound too cliché. I have no other words to describe it. Poetry is the language of symbol and sound and rhythm, and it speaks to a place within us that is hard to access through the direct, prosaic communications of everyday language. So, too, does dance. Dance is to motion what poetry is to language.

You don't have to be a dancer to appreciate the

grace of the art. You don't have to be well-versed in the technique to derive pleasure from it. Of course, a dancer is given another vehicle for self-expression, and another method of reaching out to those who are close by.

Dance is probably the primary art that is common among most cults of love and sexuality. Temple dancers have been known throughout the world, and the devadasis of India, though outlawed, still practice their sacred dancing and lovemaking in honor of Shiva.

Temple dance was documented in the ancient Middle Eastern world as well as in Egypt and Greece. In fact, the Greeks engaged in community-wide religious dances as a part of the procession to many ceremonies and as a focus of some of the rites.

In contemporary practice, a few men and women are infusing the ancient art of temple dance with a Neo-Pagan perspective. My own bellydance troupe, the Jewels of the Temple, is a small group of women practicing ritual and conveying our spirituality through the vehicle of dance and movement.

In our case, we have found the ancient rhythms and movements of bellydance (partnered with our modern twists, of course) work very well for expressing our connection to the elements, various Goddesses, and to each other. We are eclectic in our inspiration, though, and have used music from

Ireland, the Americas (including Native American drumming), Africa, India and elsewhere in our compositions. We have found that expression through the body works best for us when we release ourselves from dogmas of style and open up to the essence of the thing we are trying to dance.

Bellydance (in all of its styles) is wildly popular among Neo-Pagans because it can be so versatile and expressive, but other dance forms are worthy of exploration for those inclined to serve Aphrodite and cultivate their own grace. Lyrical dance, for instance, is a natural choice, as is modern dance. Ballet would be a good primer for these areas, and it has a composed beauty that can't be denied. Research into Greek folkloric dancing also makes a lot of sense.

EROTICISM AND SEXUALITY

Alright, I think I've established that the art of pleasure and its associated acts are not solely about erotic contact. There are more ways of giving and receiving pleasure than I've encompassed in the pages above or will be able to address in the paragraphs below. Even as that may be, I think it is an essential duty of the Priestess of Aphrodite to develop methods of giving pleasure in as many forms as possible. Eroticism and sacred sexuality are going to be a part of that.

First of all, I believe that all sex is sacred. It doesn't

have to be approached with somber gravity, as if it were a duty or chore. In fact, I think sex that is approached in that manner is less of an honor and joy to the Deities in whose names it is performed than the hot, sweaty, nearly delirious quickies that are such a vital manifestation of the true creative principle.

In fact, I hold to the idea that sex is sacred, not based solely on the fact that it is a direct representation of the act of creation. I think it's sacred, too, based on the fact that it is pleasurable and joyous. The Gods have given us these magnificent bodies that are capable of ecstatic sensations. How is that not a gift? And any gift from the Gods is automatically sacred.

So, if all sex is sacred, all consensual sexual acts are available for the repertoire of the Priestess of Aphrodite. Yes, ALL of them – as long as they are consensual. You can develop whatever proclivities you like, any methods of giving and receiving erotic pleasure.

I've mentioned before that role-playing is a fantastic tool for experiencing Divine contact during sex. I know folks who explore all of the dark pleasures of BDSM as methods of deepening their connection to Deity, as pathways for healing and as ways of showing love.

Masturbation and other acts of self-pleasuring are

almost necessary tools for this Priestesshood. If we're being honest, we can admit that all of us give ourselves pleasure. However, some of us have been taught to feel guilty or ashamed about it. These folks tend to seek a cursory release of sexual tension, and then they resent that they needed it.

How much more liberating is it to take joy in one's physicality? To enjoy one's own touch and be able to recognize it is something different than, but not necessarily lesser to, the touch of another person?

There's also a practical side to embracing the joys of self-love. If you don't play around and figure out what you like, you're going to have an exasperating time with a sex partner. If you don't luck into the right combination of touch and pressure, you'll end up dissatisfied and your partner will be confused. You may both be painfully frustrated. So, consider your personal, independent acts of sexuality to be "field research" for later practice with partners.

Really, when it comes to exploring sexual pleasures, I recommend being willing to take chances with new experiences. Play with the ways that touch and voice and environment can alter the experience. This may be the only subject of your lifelong education that you enjoy practicing so much.

EXERCISES

1. Choose an activity that you want to explore as

a study in grace and pleasure. You may already be studying this art. That's great! Just check in with yourself (in your journal) about your progress, how you feel, what discoveries you've made, and any new interests that arise from it.
2. Try something mentioned in this chapter that is outside of your comfort zone. You don't have to have an audience, but you should give it an honest try. Record your reactions/experiences in your journal.

FOR FURTHER CONSIDERATION

Nickell, Nancy. Nature's Aphrodisiacs. Crossing Press, 1999.
>This is a good place to start in your exploration of foods, drinks and herbs that inspire and induce love, passion and eroticism.

Mendelsohn, Cheryl. Home Comforts: The Art and Science of Keeping House. Scribner, 2005.
>This book may not seem sexy, but it takes the approach that a home's atmosphere is critical in making everyone in it feel comfortable. It is probably the most detailed work of its kind for understanding the ins and outs of home-making.

Greene, Robert. The Concise Art of Seduction. Profile Books, 2003.
>It may seem sneaky to talk in terms of learning the art of seduction, but we

are really talking about persuasion.
And Peitho (Persuasion), is, after all,
one of Aphrodite's daughters.
Capellanus, Andreas. <u>The Art of Courtly Love</u>.
This 12th Century handbook for lovers
describes the expectations for both the
lover and the beloved. Though standards have changed, this canonical
work explains much of the whitherto's
and wherefore's behind our concep-
tions and conventions of love and loving.

CHAPTER 9
HEIROS GAMOS

SO SAYING, HE TOOK HER BY THE HAND. AND APHRODITE, LOVER
OF SMILES,
WENT ALONG, WITH HER FACE TURNED AWAY AND HER EYES
DOWNCAST,
TOWARDS THE BED, ALL NICELY MADE, WHICH HAD ALREADY BEEN
ARRANGED FOR THE LORD,
ALL NICELY MADE WITH SOFT COVERS. AND ON TOP LAY SKINS OF
BEARS AND LIONS, WHO ROAR WITH THEIR DEEP VOICES,
WHICH HE HIMSELF HAD KILLED ON THE LOFTY MOUNTAINSIDES.
AND WHEN THEY WENT UP INTO THE STURDY BED,
HE FIRST TOOK OFF THE JEWELRY SHINING ON THE SURFACE OF HER
BODY
—THE TWISTED BROOCHES AND THE SHINY EARRINGS IN THE SHAPE
OF FLOWERS.
THEN HE UNDID HER GIRDLE AND HER RESPLENDENT GARMENTS.
HE STRIPPED THEM OFF AND PUT THEM ON A SILVER-STUDDED STOOL,
ANCHISES DID. AND THEN, BY THE WILL OF THE GODS AND BY FATE,
HE LAY NEXT TO THE IMMORTAL FEMALE, MORTAL MALE THAT
HE WAS.

- HOMERIC HYMN TO APHRODITE

The term "Heiros Gamos" means Sacred Marriage. It is specifically the term for the union of the male and female principles of divinity, though gender doesn't have to be the primary consideration in practice. Wiccans know this ritual coupling as the Great Rite. It can take form in many combinations of Deity and a mortal Priest or Priestess, but the intent is usually the same. The general purpose of the Heiros Gamos is to achieve some sort of spiritual or physical abundance.

PARTICIPANTS IN THE GREAT RITE

Greek literature is filled with examples of mortals engaging in sexual contact with Deities. Each of these examples is an instance of Sacred Marriage, and it provides us a frame of reference for examining the benefits and forms of the Rite. Spiritual enlightenment and physical abundance were among the boons bestowed on the mortals who interacted in this way with the Gods.

Middle Eastern culture and literature is also replete with Heirogamony and its sacred rites. In Sumeria and Babylon, the High Priestess would engage in ritual sex with the King once a year, usually in the spring. This was a way to unite the land (as represented by the king) with the divine (as represented by the Priestess) for the benefit of the entire community.

The above practice, the marriage of the monarch to

the land, has actually taken form in many cultures, most likely as a result of the long-standing trade routes that took so many aspects of Middle Eastern culture into the western world over the centuries. Even Celtic religious practice included rites that linked the king with the land, and the legend of Arthur – in which the land fails as the king suffers – demonstrates the power of this ancient rite.

In contemporary practice, Wiccans and Neo-Pagans participate in the Great Rite in both literal and symbolic ways. Using only symbolism, many Witchcraft Traditions end their rituals with a "penetration" of the chalice (feminine principle) by the blade (male principle). This symbolic Great Rite is typically performed as a blessing of wine, ale or some other libation that is then shared with the celebrants.

Literal practice of the Great Rite, once a staple of the Wiccan community, seems to be losing popularity as the Pagan community grows. Undoubtedly, part of the reason for this atrophy of ritual sexual magic is the fact that many Priests and Priestesses abused their power within the circle, casting a bad light not only on themselves but on the Great Rite. Another reason might be that the Wiccan and Pagan community is far more solitary now than it once was, limiting opportunities for folks to engage sexually in "perfect love and perfect trust." Yet another explanation might be that sexual practice is frightening to people, in general, and they choose not to confront their demons, if left to their own devices.

A friend of mine, a High Priest of a Wiccan coven and a long-time practitioner of the Craft, shared with me after the release of this book's first edition a little of his experience as a young man in a Wiccan coven in the late-60's and early-70's. At that time, covens didn't interact with other covens quite as freely as they do now. Often, the only Craft-folk you knew wee the ones with whom you shared oaths. "Perfect love and Perfect trust" were essential within the group. (They still are, of course, but one ran a harder gauntlet even to gain admittance into a coven back then.)

The rite his coven performed as a staple had many variations in purpose and intent, but the form often stayed the same. The High Priest and High Priestess would engage in the Great Rite while harnessing the sexual energy raised by those surrounding them in the circle. The circle-participants raised energy by pairing off in male-female partnerships and touching, kissing, etc. Contact with the genitals wasn't allowed, except for the High Priest and High Priestess. At the height of the energy, the central couple released the climactic energy for the good and goals of all. After a short break, during which the participants were free to satisfy any bodily needs they had (including personal sexual release), the ritual resumed with the remaining work according to their Tradition's format.

Most Wiccans of the 90's and 2000's would be scandalized to know that a great many of the early coven rites looked very much like this. For many now, sex and sexuality are no more a part of their spirituality or magical practices than they are in a Baptist's vacation Bible school program. So, the Great Rite has been reduced only to the symbol of the cup and the blade for most groups, with no chance of exploring the actual ecstasies of the "rite in truth."

Whatever the reasons for its current lack of popularity among the general Pagan community, the Great Rite is still a legitimate spiritual and magical practice. When covens or magical partners do choose to engage in it, the two individuals who are to be the focus of the work channel (or are possessed by) the Deities whose blessings they intend to reap. They engage in intercourse as Gods, providing bodies of flesh and blood in order for the Gods to fully enjoy the connection.

The last group of folks who enjoin themselves in the Sacred Marriage are the common people (or laymen, no pun intended) who want to experience the overflow of energy as the Priestess and King (or Priest and Priestess) invoke the Deities. They contribute their own energy to the lovemaking, and they benefit from it.

THE BOUNTY OF LOVE

Aphrodite was seen as a Goddess of fertility and of spring. One story of Her birth includes the detail that the flowers sprang to life under her feet as She stepped onto the soil of Cypress.

Love is bountiful, in terms of physical fertility as well as both emotional and spiritual boons. The Heiros Gamos is a symbolic re-enactment of the giving of all of love's blessings. These blessings include reproductive fertility in humans, animals and the land; profound religious insights; and the ecstatic physical experience of great sex.

Yes, let's not forget, please, that sex is supposed to be enjoyable. Fun, even. There's nothing wrong with being respectful of the Rite, of course, but we shouldn't be dour-faced and completely somber about it. Sex is both fun and funny, in some cases. The Gods delight in acts of joy and pleasure, after all.

A GLIMPSE, IF I MAY

The nylon tent is large enough for camping, but for the twelve or so people using it for the Sacred Marriage rite, it is snug at best. Cozy. One by one, we have taken our places in the center of the circle. One by one, we have received pleasure at each other's hands. In this ceremony, we could have engaged in intercourse, but none have done so yet. We have been waiting for Him. Breathlessly, we have been waiting for Her.

We have moistened the inside of the tent with our breath, and the air is heavy and hot. Knowing its meaning, one couple has shared water with another couple, and they really do feel the bonding that has come to be associated with that action. The air is alive and crackling with anticipation, and yet, we are at peace. The juxtaposition of tension and relaxation is a balance that we maintain without effort.

The Priest calls Him. The words are unimportant, though I recall them as poetic and powerful. His presence fills the tent and fills the man. Naked and unadorned, he becomes the raiment of the God.

Then He calls for His lover. The Priestess's eyes change first. As soon as He was with us, She started slipping in. I can see the lapis lazuli at Her throat and brow, though the woman is naked. Her straight brown hair shines with the lustrous silkiness of midnight, and stars sparkle from its depths. The smile on Her face is seductive and beguiling. I feel my own body's reactions to Her, to Him, to Them. I feel everyone else's, too. The sanctuary, a Pagan paradise, shakes with their passion. Thunder rolls across the night sky as They behold each other, these ancient lovers, and She laughed at the drums that always announce Their union.

As He took Her, and She took Him, we all watched and breathed and moaned. We felt that union, thrust for thrust. Every hungry kiss was our own.

We gave Them all that we had, and They blessed us with the outpouring of all that They are – together. The thunderstorm shook the little tent as They departed, leaving us in a hazy glow of bliss and contentment.

EXERCISES

1. A symbolic Great Rite is often used in Pagan rituals without much thought, energy or passion given to its purpose. A woman/priestess holds a cup while a man/priest dips his knife in. They say some pretty words. Everyone drinks. The end. It doesn't have to be this way. Even this symbolic hieros gamos can be filled with sensuality and cosmic connection if you allow it to be. Think about it – and actually re-enact it, either alone or with a partner. "As the cup is to the female …" That's right. Allow the cup to BE all that is feminine, receptive, welcoming, wet and warm. Really allow it to be the yoni of the Goddess. "… So the blade is to the male." Hard, piercing, penetrating, active, unrelenting. It is the God's phallus in that moment. And don't you dare just dip the tip! Allow the entire experience to overtake you. When you're ready to drink from the cup, understand that you drink the "elixir of life" – the combination of holy fluids created from the sacred marriage rite.
2. Experiment with masturbating in a meditative state. You can engage with Deity this way when

you have no partner, and you can also make offering of your love, your sex, and your energy directly to Them. Furthermore, you can make love <u>with</u> Deity in an astral form as your comfort and skill in this area increase. Aphrodite is particularly amenable to this type of working.

3. Study the art and science of invocation, find a partner whom you trust implicitly, and engage in the hieros gamos. I offer a word of caution here, though. Various traditions and magical systems teach the practice of invocation in different ways, and most urge great caution with it. I can't lightly say to jump into a possession/channeling/invocation experience to anyone who is a novice at it. <u>Learn</u> this skill and learn the safeties that surround it.

FOR FURTHER CONSIDERATION

Kraig, Donald Michael. <u>Modern Magick: Eleven Lessons in the High Magickal Arts</u>, *2 nd edition.* Llewellyn, 2002.
Kraig, Donald Michael. <u>Modern Sex Magick: Secrets of Erotic Spirituality</u>. Llewellyn, 2002.

These books are heady stuff, and they provide excellent magical background for doing everything described in this chapter. They'll also help you hone your magical steel for performing other energetic work that I haven't mentioned.

Anand, Margo and ME Naslednikov. <u>The Art of Sexual Ecstasy: The Path of Sacred Sexuality for Western Lovers.</u> Tarcher, 1989.

Anand, Margo. <u>The Art of Sexual Magic</u>. Tarcher, 1996.

These books have lots of great tips and techniques regarding sacred and magi cal sex. They also have great exercises for leading up to the hieros gamos, whether alone or with a partner.

CHAPTER 10
DARK GOLD

SHE WASHES THEIR WEAPONS WITH BLOOD AND GORE ...

HER MURDEROUS BATTLE NO ONE CAN OPPOSE - WHO RIVALS HER?

- ENHEDUANNA (OF INANNA)

All of Aphrodite's relationships teach us the many truths of love and beauty. One truth is that Aphrodite is not necessarily a Goddess entirely of light and laughter, swathed in misty pink chiffon, imbuing the world of mortals with sweetness and contentment. She has a darker side that can be quite frightening, in fact. Furthermore, Her darker aspects can teach us a great deal about the nature of love, lust, romance and beauty. Only by confronting the darkness can we truly embrace the light.

IN LOVE AND WAR

Although the much-adored Aphrodite is usually not considered a Goddess of War, She has had involvement in wars and battles. In fact, She plays a tremendous part in the Trojan War, according to legend, as one of the primary instigators of the conflict. This is reasonable when one considers that many, many wars have begun due to misplaced or misunderstood love. Even in *Romeo and Juliet*, Shakespeare has Romeo say that a particular brawl had much to do with hate, but more to do with love. These passions are closely connected, and Aphrodite is a part of them when She and Ares bring war out of love.

Apollodorus relates the most common version of the story regarding the beginnings of the Trojan War. Essentially, there was a wedding feast in honor of Peleus and Thetis, and all the Gods and Goddesses were invited – all but Strife (Eris). She "threw an apple as a prize of beauty to be contended for by Hera, Athena and Aphrodite ...." The golden apple was inscribed with the message: "Let the fair one take it." The contention between the three Goddesses, who were each considered to be surpassingly beautiful, leads to the "Judgment of Paris."

Paris, a Trojan prince, was asked by Zeus to mediate in this controversy. As a mortal man, he was given the distinct honor of pronouncing, once and for all, who was the fairest Goddess. Not surprisingly, each Goddess offered him a bribe. Aphrodite promised to give him the most beautiful woman in the world, Helen, to be his bride if he gave Her his vote. Naturally, he did so.

This was a problem because Helen was already a wife. She was married to King Menelaus, a Greek. Aphrodite sided with Paris and the Trojans in the dispute, and, throughout the long siege, She did what She could to spare the lives of certain soldiers of Troy.

Both Apollodorus and Homer describe a wound Aphrodite received on the battlefield. She was trying to help Her son, Aeneas, as he battled the fearsome Diomedes. She was wounded by Diomedes' spear in her hand after Athena had advised him to avoid all the Gods except Aphrodite. Athena said to him, "Her, at least, you may stab." The wound was inflicted where the palm meets the wrist, and it is said that the bronze spear tore through the robe the Graces had woven as well. It was at this point that She went to Dione and Zeus for comfort and was advised to tend to the affairs of marriage and leave the battlefield to others.

It may surprise some people to know that Homer, arguably Greece's earliest mythographer, did his best to demote Aphrodite from Her lofty rank among the Olympians. The earliest artifacts and legends surrounding the Goddess f Love throughout the Mediterranean cast Her as the daughter of Ouranos, the Sky, a Titan. (Zeus is the grandson of this same Titan, making Aphrodite his aunt, and possibly his elder.) Her mythos and symbolism can be traced back along the trade routes to Ishtar, the Sumerian Queen of Heaven and Earth, who is Goddess of both Love and War. In fact, all the Goddesses "descended" from Her were both sexual and warlike (Asherah, Astarte, Anat, Anahita) – until Homer revised Aphrodite.

Homer called Her the daughter to Zeus. No longer his equal (and certainly not an ancient fertility

Goddess), he went further and made her a whining weakling on the battlefield. This is a far cry from the Middle Eastern Goddesses of Love and War who had been Her progenitors. As Daniel H. Garrison points out in Sexual Culture in Ancient Greece, this is one of the reasons that Aphrodite and warlike Ares are such an ideal couple and are so naturally attracted to each other. He is literally Her other half – the warrior aspect that was stripped away when Her worship was adopted by the early Greeks.

In a few places, we can find shreds of evidence that speak to Aprhodite's intact warrior nature. In Cypress (one of the oldest islands to know Her), Corinth (where Her worship rose to its height), and Sparta (the most war-like of the Greek city-states) iconography of armed Aphrodites have been found. In these places, She was honored as a Goddess of both Love and War.

Even separated from Her war-like nature, Aphrodite is still quite capable of winning battles between great armies. She fights these battles in the heart and in the bed, though. The story of the famous "sex strike" in *Lysistrata,* in which no woman would bed any man until the war ended, is an excellent example of this power in battle.

Aphrodite's Anger

Although She is not a warrior, Aphrodite is certainly not a Goddess with whom one would wish to tangle. She is jealous of Her lovers and vengeful to any who misuse or abuse the areas of Her domain. Examples of this include using her power to punish any who slighted Her and the areas of Her domain.

Smyrna didn't honor Aphrodite, which made the Goddess very angry. So, She caused Smyrna to desire her own father sexually. Smyrna deceived him and shared his bed for twelve nights. When he discovered this, he tried to kill her. The Gods turned her into a Myrrh tree to save her life. Ten months later, the tree burst. This is how Adonis was born, and how he came into the care of Aphrodite.

Adonis was the cause for another incident that provoked the Goddess' anger. When Zeus learned of the conflict between Persephone and Aphrodite regarding the youth, He set the Muse Calliope as arbitrator. It was She who divided Adonis' year equally between the two Goddesses. Aphrodite was so enraged by this decision that She incited the Thracian women to rip Calliope's son, the famous singer Orpheus, to pieces.

Aphrodite caused Dawn to fall in love with Orion because Dawn had bedded Ares. She also caused the Sirens to grow wings because they had wished so fervently to remain virgins. Glaucus refused to let his mares breed, so She caused them to throw him during a chariot race. They ate him later.

When six of Poseidon's sons insulted Aphrodite, She struck them mad, and they gang-raped their mother. The women of Astypalaea boasted that they were more beautiful than the Goddess, and She caused them to grow cow horns. Finally, Aegus remained childless until he introduced Aphrodite's worship to Athens.

THE PRICE OF VANITY

One interpretation of the wrathful examples above could be that with Her beauty comes a certain amount of vanity and an expectation that everyone will do Her will. As the embodiment of beauty, we shouldn't be surprised that morality tales of "vanity gone wrong" are a part of the lessons She provides.

We'll notice, though, that the Goddess Herself doesn't suffer from the repercussions of vanity. She doles out judgment to mortals who overstep their bounds, while She is free from that same judgment.

LOVE, NOT ABUSE

One of the lessons that I have taken away from the stories of Aphrodite's vengeance is that She wouldn't encourage Her followers to be doormats in the name of love. Though we might do a great deal in the interest of love and friendship, we shouldn't allow ourselves to be hurt for a love that isn't reciprocal. We shouldn't be taken advantage of. We shouldn't sacrifice ourselves for someone who doesn't value that sacrifice.

Sacrifice for love that is true and returned is noble and honorable. Giving one's life or comfort for another, is an amazingly loving (if heartbreaking) act. But self-sacrificing for someone who doesn't need or appreciate the gesture is just a way of needlessly martyring oneself on the altar of love. I can't believe that Aphrodite is fond of needless sacrifice like this.

ALL IS FAIR IN LOVE AND WAR

Her wrath is not kind, and it is no wonder that so many Greek writers and historians begged for Her mercy and Her moderation. Her vengeance is terrible. Love and lust in excess are just as damaging as the ravages of war and battle.

Stalking, rape, molestation, incest, obsession – these are all examples of loving impulses gone terribly wrong. Passion can be exhilarating, but this thrill comes partially from the fact that passion is dangerous when it is unbridled. Like a caged panther, passion is thrilling to approach; but let the panther out, unleashed, and you may never get it back in the cage – and there will most certainly be some damage.

FEAR AND PANIC

As discussed earlier, Phobos and Deimos are two of

Aphrodite's children, being fathered by Ares. Love, lust and passion are often accompanied by feelings of fear and panic. In order to engage fully in acts of love, and in order to be completely immersed in love, we must overcome our fears of rejection, heartbreak, and even joy.

That's right, joy. At the core, some people are terrified of being happy. Ecstasy is a panic-inducing concept for many, no matter how much they claim to desire it. Aphrodite forces us to look deeply at ourselves facing our own darkness; and She inspires us to trust ourselves and others with our most tender parts.

DARK EROS

One titillating aspect of the darker side of Aphrodite is Her connection to the "darkly erotic." For those who are willing to explore the world of BDSM and other consensual, alternative sexual practices, part of Aphrodite's dark gold becomes tantalizingly available.

Remembering that all these acts must be consensual and adult interactions, those who choose to tread into them may have unique insights into a portion of Aphrodite's nature. Darker sexual practices, though safe in reality, give the illusion of danger – an illusion that creates an incredible sexual reaction for its participants.

These acts might include, but are certainly not limited to:

• Pain play – Using pain as a source of erotic stimulation; can use any number of methods and materials to accomplish this. Sadism is giving pain, while masochism is receiving it.

• Bondage – Tying a person up either before or after sexual acts.

• Domination and Submission – Giving up (or taking over) control of one's actions during a sexual encounter.

• Forced Fantasy – Role-playing a rape scene (that is negotiated beforehand).

One of the "safeties" that is very intricately woven into the fabric of the BDSM world is the use of a safe word. Any participant in the given scene may speak the word at any time to bring a complete halt to the activities. The word is generally a term or phrase that wouldn't normally arise in the scene – like pickle. In this way, the person who is being tied up, controlled, given pain, etc. is ultimately the person who is in control of the situation. He may stop the encounter at any point.

For all the mention I've made of BDSM, I have to admit that I have only barely flirted around the edges of its scene-work. I'm a bit of a frightened novice where BDSM is concerned. It's the panther in the cage, for me, and I am still very tentative about letting it out to roam. However, I can see the benefits that these practices can give to the folks who pursue them. After all, knowledge and experience are powerful and lead to wisdom. The knowledge and experience of Aphrodite's darker side, in a safe environment, can lead to a certain type of enlightenment regarding love, sex and beauty.

EXERCISES

1. Set aside some time to meditate on the darker aspects of Aphrodite. Be sure to journal the experiences.
2. Put pen to paper and free-associate between the concepts of "love" and "war." This can take any format you like, but if you're stuck for structures under which to do this, you can use an idea web, a flowchart, an outline, or you can just scribble random words haphazardly across the page.
3. Get out paints (or crayons or some other colorful medium) and create a depiction of one of these phrases:
   - dark gold
   - love and war
   - pain in pleasure
   - darkly erotic
   - Aphrodite of the Tombs

   Don't fret over realism or style. Focus on the colors and feelings the overall shapes evoke in you.

FOR FURTHER CONSIDERATION

Starck, Marcia and Gynne Stern. *The Dark Goddess: Dancing with the Shadow.* Crossing Press, 1993.
>This is a fabulous book for the beginning exploration of Dark Goddess energy. Of particular interest to Aphrodisians will be the sections on Inanna (a pre-cursor to Aphrodite) and Medusa (on of Aphrodite's priestesses, according to legend).

Miller, Philip and Molly Devon. Screw the Roses, Send Me the Thorns: The Romance and Sexual Sorcery of Sadomasochism. Mystic Rose Books, 1988.
>This is a classic book on BDSM, and it is a great starting place for those interested in taking a peak into the world of the "darkly erotic."

CHAPTER 11
THE TEMPLE, RENEWED

COME, O COME, DIVINEST SHELL,

AND IN MY EAR ALL THY SECRETS TELL.

SAPPHO

The temples to the Goddesses of Love are being rebuilt through the hearts and hands of the faithful. I can see that discussions are happening with both online and offline groups that are more deeply exploring the worship and wisdom of Aphrodite, Ishtar, Astarte, and so on. The Priests and Priestesses of sacred loving are more and more visible within the larger Pagan community, offering workshops at festivals, training in their locales, and online communications with any who would join in.

Sappho wrote, "I yearn and I seek." Like so many, I long for the openness and sharing of conversations, rituals and training in the art and insights of sacred sexuality. I seek out that information and experience, and I am ready, at long last, to make my own contributions to the body of wisdom and practice.

I am also in search of resources that broaden my perspective regarding Aphrodite and Her worship in all aspects.

FINDING THE RESOURCES

For this type of work, I heartily believe that seeking out the practical, experiential resources is of the highest value. You can only theorize for so long.

The list of groups' websites listed in the Appendix, then, is intended as a means for you to find groups of real people who are actually meeting somewhere to work with Aphrodite, sacred sexuality or one of the other related topics. These groups meet according to their own calendars and needs, and some still in a place only to offer online experience. In time, though, more and more opportunities and communities will surface for seekers interested in this work.

STARTING YOUR OWN GROUP

Yes, you may find that you need to begin your own local Cult of Aphrodite (ritual group), thiasos (learning and discussion group), damos (community), or even establish a temenos (temple) to Aphrodite. You may find that a Sacred Touch Circle (sacred sexuality group) meets your needs as a devotee of Aphrodite. Founding your own group is a valid way of discovering the wisdom and Mysteries of Aphrodite Most Lovely.

Of course, you'll need to consider a few points before you begin:

Location – You'll need a meeting place if you're going to have real-world interactions. Consider privacy, comfort, capacity, driving distance, décor. When you find a location that you can afford and that meets most of your needs, be realistic about how you can compensate for the locale's shortcomings and play up its perks. You'll probably need to prioritize regarding the qualities of the site that are most important to you, at least in the beginning. For example, if you plan on doing a great deal of sacred sexual work in temple space, privacy and comfort will likely rank highly on your list. You may not need the capacity to hold more than a four or five people, though, so a guest bedroom in your home could work quite nicely.

Frequency – Are you going to meet on a regular basis? Weekly, bi-weekly, monthly? Or does it make more sense to you to investigate and create a festival schedule for your rituals and workings? There really is no right or wrong answer here, but you may find that your group has its own "right" frequency of meetings. When you meet too often, the group starts to develop a sense of burnout. Meeting too infrequently leads to feeling disconnected. Be open to changing the schedule based on the needs of the particular group of people who come to share this celebration with you.

Exclusivity – Will you have membership requirements of some sort? How well do you need to know

your participants before they are allowed to participate fully? If you are working with sexuality at all,
what, if anything, do you need to know about your
members' sexual histories or STD status? If you
choose to work with a small, closed group, will you
offer any opportunities for new people who may be
interested in joining you (like workshops or public
rituals)?

Roles – We discussed various types of Priests and
Priestesses in Chapter 3. Which of these roles do
you need for the work you intend to do? How many
of the roles are you capable of filling on your own?
How will you compensate for those roles that are
not your expertise? You may find that you are all
too willing to be the chief cook and bottle-washer,
but you don't have to do everything on your own in
order for the group to run smoothly. In fact, it may
run much more smoothly if you learn to delegate.
Recognize and develop talent where it grows within
your community, and everyone will benefit.

Safer Sex Practices – If you are considering any
form of sacred sexual practice, you need to adopt
safer sex practices to be used without fail during
group workings. Latex gloves, condoms and lubri-
cant need to be present for everyone all the time.
Nobody should be touching anyone else's genitals
without a layer of latex. The only exception to this
rule would be in the case of fluid-bonded partners
(spouses or other long-term, committed lovers). We
all know it feels physically better without the con-

dom, but the overall safety of the group and its members is a much higher priority. Everyone's going to feel a lot worse (physically and psychologically) if the group manages to share an STD.

Tools and Toys – You can really add any type of accoutrement that you like. Appeal to your aesthetics – and those of your group-mates – in outfitting your rituals and workings. Look to the ancients for ideas. Look to your contemporaries. Look in the sex toy shops, if you feel inclined.

Content – What kind of work are you going to do together? How will you go about creating lessons or rituals? Again, this comes back to your "vision" for the group. What are you trying to accomplish together? Is it a study group, a social community, a ritual group, a sacred sex circle? Is it a temple that incorporates all of these things?

Like the rest of us who are taking up the work of Aphrodite (and the other Goddesses of Love and Sexuality), you will be pioneering your own way. As our work grows and expands, we will have more contact with each other and more opportunity to engage in public discussions. We will be able to learn and work with each other on a more regular basis, and possibly on a larger scale.

SEEKERS/DEVOTEES

With this type of temple (or community) you're going to have individuals who come to you with a desire to be close to Aphrodite, but they may have no real interest in participating in the festivals or studying the myths. Indeed, such a person may come to you, your community, or your temple for any number of reasons, not the least of which is being near an embodiment of Aphrodite.

If you embrace and enhance Her qualities, as we've discussed throughout this book, people may be drawn to you simply because they can reach Aphrodite more easily while in you presence. If this happens – before this happens – you need to take stock of your comfort level for "standing in" for the Goddess in the many ways you may face.

Are you willing and able to …

> … speak the words of the Lady as She says them in your ear?
> … reach out and touch a seeker/devotee in comfort, joy and passion?
> … invoke Aphrodite and allow Her to move through you freely?
> … make love with a devotee, whether invoked or not, as appropriate to the working or celebration at hand?
> … lead rituals in celebration of Her, for private or public attendance?

Right now, you may not be willing or trained to do all of these things. Perhaps some items on the list will always be off-limits to you. However, you may find that as you open yourself to Her experience, to Her touch, that you are wiling and able to do whatever task She presents in the form of a devotee on your doorstep.

TRAINING/TEACHING

At some point, men and women may come to you asking for guidance in a more vocational application. They may recognize in you what they want to become themselves, and they'll ask for your help in becoming Priests or Priestesses in their own rights.

This is both a challenge and a blessing. At this point in my own life, I've taught a number of things at very intense levels – literature and composition (to public high school students), theatre and speech (to more high school students), bellydance (to adult women), witchcraft (to my coven and at workshops), and now the Aphrodisian arts. I find that a few key concepts are usually true of good teachers, regardless of location, subject or level.

First, a good teacher absolutely **must** be knowledgeable regarding the topic. Before you agree to teach another person how to be a Priestess of Aphrodite, make sure you're honest with yourself about how much you really know about it. More than that, make sure you're honest with your would-be student.

The truth is: this was a dormant Priestesshood that we are reviving. How much do any of us really know about it? What training have we received? Not much. We can pilfer through books, look at artifacts, make some educated guesses, and then jump right into the work. If we are brave and ready to do what we hear Aphrodite saying to do, this first generation of Priests and Priestesses will learn through practical experience more than anything else. So, when I say, "Be knowledgeable," for now that means that you'll want to have some intellectual understanding of myth and history, but, more importantly, you'll want to have enough practical experience working with Aphrodite and Her devotees to feel comfortable guiding others in the same pursuits.

Second, a good teacher is passionate about the subject matter. To teach well, you've really got to love the topic. In our case, I think that means really honoring, accepting, and being devoted to Aphrodite. I think those who will end up showing others how to do what we do are going to burn so brightly with Her flame that they will be unable to keep themselves from sharing what they do with those around them.

Third, the best teachers are invested in their students. The holy triad of teaching could be said to be the information, the teacher and the student. Each is equally important to the process, and if the teacher doesn't respect and honor the student, the process is doomed to failure. That respect includes showing compassion, understanding, and patience with the student as she struggles, as well as demonstrating joy and interest and pride as she succeeds. Many of the challenges and successes of the student are ones the teacher has already faced, making it all too easy to diminish them as insignificant or minor, but this is a disservice to the student and the process of growth.

Finally, the best teachers have usually identified their personally teaching philosophies. In fact, in the world of teacher preparation, novice teachers are encouraged to sit down and write a document that details their philosophical approaches to the learning process. The document addresses your beliefs about what it means to learn – whether learning a fact, a theory, a method, a process, a skill, or something entirely different – and how you feel about the learning process. Furthermore, to teach, it isn't enough to understand how "you" learn, you need to understand how others learn so you can develop some methods for reaching others in a style in which they're actually likely to retain and use the information that has been taught.

Your "training program" will flow rather naturally out of your philosophy and the goals you have for sharing the subject with your particular students.

FINAL THOUGHTS

This book is my small offering to those who feel drawn to Aphrodite and Her worship. I know that there is more to discuss, explore, and share. I haven't tried to create a comprehensive guide to Aphrodisian ritual and theology, and I hope other practitioners will come forward with their own contributions to answer some of the questions I've had to leave unanswered.

In the meantime, I hope that you experience Aphrodite deeply and lovingly in your personal work.

EXERCISES

1. How do you feel about working within a temple, cult, thiasos or damos? Are you willing to help start one? Would you rather work on your own?
2. Explore your reactions to the discussion on working with seekers/devotees. How open do you feel right now to the idea of working with those who seek Aphrodite in and through you?
3. Start sketching your learning philosophy. Whether or not you intend to teach others in the near (or distant) future, this may be a helpful tool for you in mapping out your own training as you seek to grow a Priestess.

FOR FURTHER CONSIDERATION

Amber K. <u>Coven Craft: Witchcraft for Three or</u>

<u>More</u>. Llewellyn, 2002.

> Really details the ups and downs of forming a Pagan spiritual group in a contemporary context. Takes a Wiccan approach, but very useful for anyone leading a working group today.

APPENDIX

BIBLIOGRAPHIC RESOURCES

NEO-PAGAN PRINCIPLES AND PRACTICES

Farrar, Janet and Stewart with Gavin Bone. *The Witches' Way: Principles, Rituals and Beliefs of Modern Witchcraft*. Phoneix Publishing, 1986.
>   Basic introduction to witchcraft and Neo-Paganism. Isn't so Trad-specific as to be bothersome for the new Pagan.

Valiente, Doreen. An ABC of Witchcraft Past and Present. Phoenix Publishing, 1985.
>   A classic work on older Craft practice.

GREEK RELIGION, HELLENISMOS AND APHRODITE

Apollodorus. Library and Epitome, 6th Ed.. JG Frazer, ed. Loeb Classics, 1960.

Burkert, Walter. Greek Religion. Basil Blackwell and Harvard University Press, 1985.
>   As mentioned within this work's text, this book is one of the contemporary classics dealing with ancient/Classical Greek religion. Anyone seriously interested in the topic should have a copy of this book for reference.

Empedocles. Porphyrius de Abstinentia. Trans. By Frederick John Kluth. http://www.fjkluth.com/aphro.html.

Hesiod. Theogony, Works and Days. ML West, ed. and trans. Oxford University Press, 1999.

Hesiod and HG Evelyn White. Hesiod: The Homeric Hymns and Homerica. Loeb Classics, 1914.

Homer. The Iliad of Homer. Richard Lattimore, ed. University of Chicago Press, 1961.

Paris, Ginette. Pagan Meditations: The Worlds of Aphrodite, Artemis and Hestia. Continuum, 1991.
Beautiful work with reflections on the three Goddesses covered.

Pausanais. Descriptions of Greece.
This ancient, but secondary, source describes statuary and other pieces of art in Greece. It has some analysis of and relevance to more ancient work – like Hesiod and Homer.

Pindar. Odes. ed. Diane Svarlien. 1990.

Reif, Jennifer. Mysteries of Demeter: Rebirth of the Pagan Way. Weiser, 2000.
Practical and informative introduction to Neo-Hellenic practice – specifically, Goddess-based.

SEXUALITY — SACRED AND OTHERWISE

Anand, Margo. The Art of Sexual Ecstasy. Tarcher, 1989.

> As mentioned within the body of this work, both of Anand's titles are helpful for exploring sacred sex. They take a Western approach to Eastern Tantra.

Anand, Margo. The Art of Sexual Magic. Tarcher, 1996.

Easton, Dossie and Catherine A. Liszt. The Ethical Slut: A Guide to Infinite Sexual Possibilities. Greenery Press, 1997.

> This is book has been eye-opener for many who have been trapped by conventional ideas of "promiscuity." It is a basic treatise on polyamory – the ability to love more than one person at the same time.

Easton, Dossie and Janet W. Hardy. *The* New Bottoming Book. Greenery Press, 2001.

> Both titles by these authors open readers to ideas of the "darkly erotic."

Easton, Dossie and Janet W. Hardy. The New Topping Book. Greenery Press, 2003.

SPIRITUAL RESOURCES

Cult of Aphrodite Pelagia
http://cultofaphrodite.org/
This group is based in the foothills of the Si-

erra Nevada range in northern California. They work together on a regular basis, in addition to presenting rituals and workshops in California.

Thiasos Aphrodite

http://groups.yahoo.com/thiasos_aphrodite
This is my own online organization, a loose confederacy of people drawn to learn about and work with Aphrodite. Though this is primarily an online forum, it is a good place to begin the search for like-minded individuals. We have a related yahoo group for discussion, as well.

Cult of Aphrodite Asteria

http://groups.yahoo.com/aphrodite_asteria
Based in Southern Indiana, this is a working mystery cult associated with Aphrodite. I am the Hiereia of this group, and we use a festival calendar that we have developed for working with the Kyprian throughout the year. Some rituals are private, some are open to the public, and some are held in individual devotion. In the near future, we will officially establish the Temple of Aphrodite Asteria, which will feature regular publication of a sacred sexuality journal, hierodule training on- and off-line, and more.

Hellenismos: Hellenic Polytheist Blogs and Forum

http://hellenismos.us
Maintained by Timothy Alexander, this is one of the most direct and comprehensive sites deal-

ing with functional, practical (and not merely theoretical) Neo-Hellenic practice.

Temenos Theon

http://kyrene.4t.com/index.html

This sacred space on the web boasts a cache of information from Classical and contemporary sources. This is a valuable library for beginners and advanced practitioners, alike.

Qadishti Community

http://www.qadishti.org

Based in Cincinnati and led by Michael A. Manor, the Qadishti Institute sponsors this community of sacred sex practitioners, and it values practice over theory in sacred sexual workings. QI offers a program of training that includes mini-tracks at festivals and celebrations. QI is associated with the Roman Caesarean Church and the Temple of Venus Erycina, and it hosts the website and forum listed above.

Temple of the Red Lotus

http://www.templeredlotus.com/index.htm

Based in Atlanta, GA, this temple recognizes and promotes the sanctity of sex, the body, love, relationships and more. The Temple and Inara de Luna, its founder, present workshops throughout the Southwest, and they also sponsor live chats with pioneers in sacred loving. Finally, Red Lotus offers comprehensive qadishtu training for those interested in exploring that calling.

Terra Incognita
mailto:oryter@yahoo.com

Terra Incognita doesn't have an online face for the temple, but its founders can be reached via e-mail, and they participate actively in the sacred sexuality community. TI is a qadishtu temple, training temple harlots and temple dogs (a term sometimes used for male priests/ guards). They engage with seekers in everything from sincere non-sexual counsel to deeply connected courtesan-like relationships. Their goal is to help integrate a seekers mind, body and spirit in a healthy way.

Aphrodite's Temple
www.ravenslairleather.com

This particular temple of Aphrodite is located in central Texas and run by Gigi Raven Wilbur. It is a sacred sexuality temple that offers training opportunities to priest/ess prostitutes and integrated healing opportunities to seekers.

There are a few other groups out there, but most come in the form of online communities for discussion, and very few offer live, real-time, in-person rituals or classes. However, by checking out the websites and e-mail groups above, you may be able to find links that lead you to a particular area of your own interest within the world of Aphrodisian service and discussion. You may also find the support you need to start your own group.

LEGAL RESOURCES

LAWS

ProCon.org – Prostitution Laws and Related Punishments

http://www.prostitutionprocon.org/law.htm

A comprehensive listing of Federal, State and Local laws regarding prostitution. The parent site presents a well-researched, non-biased forum for the exploration of the issue of prostitution.

ADVOCACY

Network of Sex Work Projects

http://www.nswp.org/

Informal alliance of sex workers and organizations that provides services to sex workers. Member groups in more than 40 countries. Focused on health and human rights.

SEX WORK, SEXUAL HEALING AND SEX COUNSELING

International Sex Worker Foundation for Art, Culture and Education

http://www.iswface.org/about.html

An educational resource center that promotes and preserves the art and culture created by and about sex workers.

International Union of Sex Workers
http://www.iusw.org/
Campaigns for the human, civil and labor rights of sex workers around the world.

$pread Magazine
http://www.spreadmagazine.org/
Magazine for sex workers aimed at representing the industry (and its workers) accurately, building a community, and destigmatizing sex work by providing a forum for its individual and diverse voices.

American Association of Sexuality Educators, Counselors and Therapists
http://www.aasect.org
This is an interdisciplinary professional organization that includes individuals who are interested in promoting understanding of human sexuality and healthy sexual behavior. This group provides its members with networking opportunities as well options for professional education, growth, and development.

Sexual Healers and Educators Guild
http://
www.sexualhealersandeducatorsguild.com
This organization promotes a loving, joyous and conscious world through sex-positive education and coaching. The focus of most of the practi-

APPENDIX 🌿

tioners offering services through this site is Tantric.

179

ABOUT THE AUTHOR

Laurelei Black is a founding High Priestess of the Spiral Castle Tradition of Witchcraft and is a student of 1734 and Thelema. In addition to her service to Aphrodite, Laurelei is also a devoted Priestess of Tubal Qayn. She is a participating member of the Qadishti Movement and is the Hiereia of the Cult of Aphrodite Asteria.

Laurelei lives with her crazy-wonderful family in Indiana.

17338756R00112

Made in the USA
Middletown, DE
20 January 2015